SKI SUNDAY

Over the top at Wengen

SKI SUNDAY
John Samuel

British Broadcasting Corporation

John Samuel has been covering the Winter Olympic Games and international skiing for The Guardian *since 1964, and has been Sports Editor since 1968. He is a keen skier himself and has written two books on the subject:* Love of Skiing *and* Ski-wise. *He has been the BBC's consultant on winter sports since 1968.*

Published by the
British Broadcasting Corporation
35 Marylebone High Street
London W1M 4AA

ISBN 0 563 17992 9

First published 1982
© The British Broadcasting Corporation
and the Contributors 1982

Printed in England
by Jolly & Barber Ltd,
Rugby, Warwickshire

CONTENTS

Picture credits

Page 1 Bild & News; 3 Colorsport; 4 Kenneth Saunders; 12 Keystone Zurich; 13 Salomon (GB) Ltd; 16 Popperfoto (UPI/D. Hespe); 17 *top* Schweizerische Radio– und Fernsehgesellschaft, *bottom* Fremdenverkersverband Kitzbuehel; 21 *top left* Konrad Bartelski, *top right* Keystone Zurich, *bottom* Pressebildagentur Werek; 24 Russell/Kelly; 25 Popperfoto (UPI/Erwin Wyrsch); 26, 27 Ski Racing; 29 Colorsport; 30 *left* Keystone Zurich, *right* Bild & News; 31 Keystone Zurich; 32 Colorsport; 35 Peter Freithofer, *inset* Konrad Bartelski; 37 *top* Keystone Zurich (Foschini); 37 *bottom*, 40 Salomon (GB) Ltd; 42 Sport & General; 44 All Sport (*top left*, Steve Powell, *bottom* Tony Duffy), *top right* Keystone Zurich; 45 All Sport (*top left & bottom* Tony Duffy, *top right* Don Morley); 46 *left* All Sport (Tony Duffy), *right* Canadian Ski Association; 48 *top* Keystone Zurich, *bottom* All Sport (Tony Duffy); 49 *left* Bild & News, *right* Colorsport; 51 *top* Central Press (ASL), *bottom* Peter Pospisil; 52 *top* All Sport (Rauch), *bottom* Salomon (GB) Ltd; 53 Keystone Zurich (AFP); 55 Popperfoto (UPI/D. Hespe); 56 *top* Keystone Zurich, *bottom* Salomon (GB) Ltd; 57 Keystone Zurich (Foschini); 59 *left* Konrad Bartelski, *right* All Sport (Don Morley); 60, 61 Colorsport; 61 *inset* Konrad Bartelski; 62 *inset* David Vine; 63 BBC Television; 65 Bildarchiv Hans Huber; 67 Hunter Mountain Ski Bowl News Bureau (Paul E. Pele); 68 Killington Ski Resort (Bob Perry); 73 BBC (Geoff Goode); 77 Colorsport; 79 Office du Tourisme Municipal de Val d'Isère; 81 Colorsport; 85 Daniel Rose; 89 All Sport (MM); 90 Keystone Zurich (Euler); 93 Konrad Bartelski; 96 Russell/Kelly; 99 Colorsport; 100, 101 Russell/Kelly (Carl Yarbrough); 103 Daniel Rose; 104 Bild & News; 105 Russell/Kelly (Carl Yarbrough); 106 All Sport (Tony Duffy); 108, 109 Daniel Rose; 110 Popperfoto (UPI/Diane Huntress); 111 Daniel Rose; 112 J. Allan Cash; 113 Daniel Rose; 115 Konrad Bartelski; 116, 120, 121 Daniel Rose; 123 John Samuel; 125 Colorsport; 126 *inset* BBC Picture Library; 128 *top* All Sport (Don Morley), *bottom* Colorsport; 132 Philip Cayford.

ALL SPORT: 135 Buergler (Don Morley), 138 P. Mahre (Steve Powell); KONRAD BARTELSKI: 135 Enn, 136 Gruber, 138 Mueller, Orlainsky, Podborski, 139 Ortner, Read, 140 A. Wenzel, Zhirov, 142 Fisher, 143 Moesenlechner, 144 Walliser, 145 H. Wenzel; BILD & NEWS: 137 Luethy, 141 de Agostini; BULGARISCHER SKIVERBAND: 139 Popangelov; CANADIAN SKI ASSOCIATION: 137 Irwin, 144 Sorensen; COLORSPORT: 135 de Chiesa, 136 Grissmann, 138 Noeckler, 142 Kinshofer; DEUTSCHER SKIVERBAND: 141 M. Epple; A.J. GELSSER PRESSEBILD: 142 Nelson; KEYSTONE, ZURICH: 136 Fournier, Gaspoz (J.P. Froidevaux), Gros, 137 Klammer, 138 Mally, 139 Spiess, Stenmark (Pressensbild Stockholm/K. Jonasson), 140 Stock, Walcher, Wirnsberger (all Votavafoto Vienna), 143 Konzett; POPPERFOTO: 135 Andreev (UPI/NTB), 136 Fjaellberg (Pressensbild Stockholm/L. Groth), Frommelt (UPI/K. Heirler), Girardelli (UPI/Bild & News – E. Wyrsch), 137 Halsnes (UPI/J. Schmitt), Krizaj (AFP/Aigles), 138 S. Mahre (UPI/K. Heirler), 139 Pfaffenbichler (UPI/J. Marquette), 140 Strel (UPI/Bild & News – E. Wyrsch), Tsyganov (UPI/J. Marquette), Weirather (UPI/K. Heirler), 141 Bieler (UPI/J. Marquette), Cooper (UPI), I. Epple (UPI/Sanden), 142 Flanders (UPI/Sanden), Hess (UPI), Kirchler (UPI/J. Marquette), 143 Patrakeeva, Pelen (both UPI/L. Mellace), 144 Proell (UPI/Sanden), Quario, Serrat (both UPI/L. Mellace), 145 Zini (E. Wyrsch); PETER POSPISIL: 141 Charvatova: SALOMON (GB) LTD: 137 Hoflehner; SKI RACING: 143 McKinney (E. Pickett).

Maps and diagrams by Line and Line.

FOREWORD

BBC Television has been featuring skiing in its sports programmes with increasing regularity since the 1964 Winter Olympic Games in Innsbruck. Great champions like triple gold medallist Jean-Claude Killy and Austria's downhill star Franz Klammer have provided us with moments of excitement that stand in the memory, alongside the great moments of any sport. Klammer's victory in front of his home crowd at the 1976 Olympic Games ranked as one of the television sporting occasions of the decade for sheer excitement.

Despite limited British participation at the top level, the British audience has shown its appreciation and interest in increasing numbers. For the past four seasons, skiing has had a series of its own, 'Ski Sunday', and millions of viewers, many of whom have never ventured near the ski slopes, have made a regular Sunday teatime date to watch the world's best ski-racers do battle on the snowy tightrope that often separates success from crashing disaster.

What is the growing appeal of a sport that Britons can claim to have invented but in which they now rarely feature at the top? One factor is surely the rapidly improving quality of the television pictures produced by our European broadcasting colleagues, with modern, small lightweight cameras which can be more skilfully positioned to capture the spectacular and dramatic downhill sweeps of the most daunting 'pistes' on the circuit. These clean, crisp – and often sunny – pictures provide a breath of fresh air in British midwinter and, of course, the competitors themselves are the best skiers in the world, providing the best possible competition. And for almost a million of us who now go skiing each year – and for whom the sight of a fresh fall of snow has a unique and special excitement – the programme is a welcome reminder of the pleasures and challenges we find on the snow and in the mountains.

This book is about the racers – how they race and the background to their sport. John Samuel, *The Guardian*'s Sports Editor and an expert winter sports journalist who has been involved with skiing and television since the sixties, has edited and compiled it and written many of the chapters. Expert commentators

David Vine and Ron Pickering take you behind the scenes, as does Britain's leading skier, Konrad Bartelski, who has contributed and advised in a number of technical areas. We would also like to thank the Canadian downhiller, Ken Read, Matthew Fisher of the Canadian Broadcasting Corporation, Divina Galica, the former British Olympic skier, now a racing driver, and Alan Smith, winter sports correspondent of the *Daily Telegraph*, for their contributions.

We hope this book will be a valuable aid to the growing number of ski fans, whether they get their fun vicariously through the medium of the television screen, or in person on the slopes. If it also encourages some viewers out of their armchairs to try the sport for themselves, then the enthusiastic team that brings you 'Ski Sunday' will be more than delighted.

Jonathan Martin
Head of Sport/BBC Television

BBC TELEVISION'S PLANNED SKI COVERAGE 1981–82

Wed 2 December	Sportsnight	Val d'Isère	Women's downhill
Sat 5 December	Grandstand	Val d'Isère	Men's downhill & GS
Sat 12 December	Grandstand	Piancavallo	Women's downhill & slalom
Sun 13 December	*Ski Sunday*	Val Gardena	Men's downhill
Sat 19 December	Grandstand	Bad Kleinkircheim	Women's downhill (2)
Sun 20 December	*Ski Sunday*	Crans-Montana	Men's downhill
Fri 1 January	Grandstand	Garmisch	Four Hills Jumping
Sun 3 January	*Ski Sunday*	Innsbruck	Four Hills Jumping
		Maribor	Women's slalom
Sat 9 January	Grandstand	Morzine	Men's Downhill
Sun 10 January	*Ski Sunday*	Morzine	Men's slalom
Wed 13 January	Sportsnight	Grindelwald	Women's downhill
Sat 16 January	Grandstand	Kitzbuehel	Men's downhill
Sun 17 January	*Ski Sunday*	Kitzbuehel	Men's slalom
Wed 20 January	Sportsnight	Bad Gastein	Women's downhill
Sat 23 January	Grandstand	Wengen	Men's downhill
Sun 24 January	*Ski Sunday*	Wengen	Men's slalom
Thu 28 January	Sportsnight		
to	Grandstand	Schladming	World Championships
Sun 7 February	*Ski Sunday*		
Sat 13 February	Grandstand	Garmisch	Men's downhill
Sun 14 February	*Ski Sunday*	Garmisch	Men's slalom
Wed 3 March	Sportsnight	Oslo	World 90m Jumping Championships

Grandstand and Sportsnight are on BBC 1. *Ski Sunday* is on BBC 2; most of its programmes will include highlights from the previous day also.

1

THE MAKING
OF THE WHITE CIRCUS

John Samuel

The World Cup was set up in 1967 to reward the world's best ski racers. Naively, it might seem fifteen years later, it meant reward only in the sense of achievement on the slopes. The idea simply was to give a points system and a better identity to the ramshackle circuit of International Ski Federation (FIS) races run independently by resorts and clubs. Some were classic events – the Arlberg–Kandahar, rotating among the top resorts of St Anton, Chamonix and Garmisch, the Hahnenkamm at Kitzbuehel, and the Lauberhorn at Wengen. Others were as temporary as tents in a blizzard, but the illusion of a travelling sporting entertainment grew rather than faded. The White Circus, 'La Cirque Blanche', had truly arrived.

'World Cup' was a piece of badge engineering thought up by a sharp-minded Swiss-French journalist from Alsace, Serge Lang, one of whose employers, *L'Equipe*, a sporting newspaper centred on Paris, had helped start the cycling Tour de France and the motor-racing Grand Prix circuit. Evian, the French mineral water firm, came in as joint sponsors, to be succeeded eventually by Seven.Up. For soccer fans, the very term World Cup was misleading, representing more a knock-out competition. The ski World Cup was in truth a league for individuals travelling under national team banners and finance. Quickly the idea gained the support of two of the most influential team directors, Honoré Bonnet of France and Bob Beattie of the USA. John Fry, another journalist, then editor of the US *Ski* magazine, came in with an associated Nations Cup, for team results, and the scheme rapidly took off. FIS at times seemed a bit bemused by it all. A largely self-elected body, centred on Berne, with four executive vice-presidents and a general council of twelve, plus secretary-general, it was dominated then as now by Marc Hodler, its multi-lingual Swiss president.

Hodler, under his other hat, the treasurership of the International Olympic Committee (IOC), shared the general commitment to keep skiing as a member of the Olympic family. Lang often derided the Games, but as the years went by Olympism moved nearer the World Cup rather than vice-versa. Hodler must take most of the credit for keeping skiing and the Olympics together. Most national

teams originally were funded by governments concerned with Olympic medal prestige, and such commercialisation that existed in the early days was on a limited scale. All but the very top skiers were amateurs in fact as well as name, including even the French, although Gaullist France heavily funded the national squad. The two outstanding targets were Olympic and World Championship gold medals – awarded simultaneously – and the World Championships themselves held every fourth year between Games. After virtually a clean sweep of the world championship medals at Portillo in 1966 it was no surprise that the French were keen on other ways of exploiting their national team and their burgeoning resort industry. Latecomers in the game, they were busily developing resorts at altitude.

They had applied successfully for Grenoble as the site of the 1968 Winter Olympic Games, and to an already strong hand they were dealt an ace – Jean-Claude Killy, an athlete of perceptive, innovating mind and lean, haunted good looks. His three gold medals at Grenoble followed two glittering years when he won the two opening World Cup competitions. If the World Cup cannot be said to have made Killy, then Killy certainly made the World Cup. Today, thirteen years after his last amateur race, he remains the best-known skiing personality in North America. His Rolls-Royce Silver Cloud sits most of the time in a Geneva garage. In 1981 a TV interviewer was asking, 'When is your next race?'

At the Grenoble Games Killy, garlanded with three gold medals, sold his picture to *Paris Match* for £3000, enrolled with Mark McCormack, and became the first ski-racing millionaire. Endorsements were the name of an important game in a quickly expanding industry. Killy helped sell everything, from credit cards to cameras. America's skiers were challenged to try and beat him under a handicap system and McCormack sold the deal to television. Killy came just at the right time for TV. So did the World Cup. But everyone, television included, still wanted the Olympic Games, and the Winter Games without the top skiers was unthinkable. Not everyone could make it up Mount McCormack like Killy.

A major crisis came when Avery Brundage, president of the IOC, expelled Austria's leading skier, Karl Schranz, from the 1972 Winter Olympics in Sapporo. He was, said Brundage, the most blatant and verbose of critics. Schranz's words, given to Will Grimsley, sports editor of Associated Press, on the practice slopes of Sapporo, were of historic importance in sport. He refused to confirm or deny reports of an income of £20,000 a year from equipment endorsements and other off-snow activities, but said:

I don't think it matters where a man's money comes from. This should not enter into the Olympics in any way. This thing of amateur purity is something that dates back to the nineteenth century when amateur sportsmen were regarded as gentlemen and everyone else was an outcast. The Olympics should be a competition of skill and strength and speed – no more. If we followed Mr Brundage to the true end then the Olympics would be only for the very rich . . . We should judge sportsmen simply as people, rich or poor, black or white, and they should be rewarded according to what they accomplish. That should be the real spirit of the Olympics, and some day that's the way it will be.

Brundage, like the battered old battleship he was, never struck his flag. 'There is no moral justification in building a ski run and cable car for millions of dollars on Mount Eniwa and turning them over for demolition tomorrow,' he said. 'Ski racing depends too much on its equipment and its facilities to be an Olympic sport.' The world, it seemed, thought differently. Sapporo was happy to be established as the principal winter sports city of the Orient. Five million dollars for one vanishing ski run (it was the only mountain with the vertical drop for a downhill) was peanuts beside it.

A crowd of a quarter of a million turned out for Schranz's premature home-coming to Vienna. The son of an Arlberg railway tunnel worker who died from the soot in his lungs, Schranz was now a national hero. Times were changing, and the World Cup which he was to win in 1969 and 1970 was changing with them. It was rarely without stress and controversy.

Partly in the wake of the Schranz affair, the IOC at its 1974 congress, by sheer coincidence in Vienna, changed its rules to permit athletes of all descriptions to be paid for lost earnings. Skiers were not entirely off the hook if they wished to continue competing in Olympics. The money which makers of skis, boots, suits, gloves and goggles were panting to pay racers had to be laundered through national federations. Effectively, it meant that top racers need never want for the present, and their futures were guaranteed.

Austria, Italy, Switzerland and France went about things in different ways. The French had a huge family row. Georges Joubert, professor of ski at Grenoble University, sacked six top skiers when he was appointed to succeed Bonnet, and France disappeared as a men's ski-racing force for a ski generation. On the other hand, Joubert and a former Olympic champion, Juan Vuarnet, winner of the 1960 downhill at Squaw Valley, employed knowledge of racer techniques, and in particular *avalement* or 'the sharp retraction of the knees and shooting forward of the feet at the start or finish of a turn', to exploit the new French teaching methods. Austria introduced yet another new national system; Switzerland offered a middle way, combining learning techniques of both rivals. The Italians poured money into the ski team and experimented successfully with better equipment. Racer techniques, rejected in the fifties as hopelessly arcane for the once-a-year holidaymaker, were incorporated into glossy tourist packages as each Alpine nation vied for the booming ski market. In truth, with major improvements in ski and boot design, younger, fitter people could be taught to ski well in a fortnight. With the anorak de rigueur from Aberdeen to Abitone, TV pouring the thrills and spills of World Cup racing into living-rooms across Europe, the bits and pieces came together for a multi-billion-dollar industry.

Women have never lagged far behind men in skiing. Nancy Greene, Canada's pioneer World Cup winner, earned as much criticism from Mr Brundage as anyone else. It was a woman, Annemarie Moser-Proell, whose identification with her skis more clearly demonstrated the validity of the endorsement game than anyone else. The Alpine countries absorb racers in a variety of roles. Karl

Karl Schranz: expelled from the Olympics, but a hero in Vienna

Schranz is head of the St Anton ski school, the most famous in the world. Modern French resorts like to associate with a famous racer or coach. But mostly the trade wants identification with current winners. Annemarie was spotted in 1970 by a small-town Austrian ski maker, Alois Rohrmoser, as a 13-year-old 'wunderkind' on wooden skis with cable bindings. Then he was making 32,000 Atomic skis a year. It was 700,000 by the time Annemarie came through with six World Cup titles and, finally in 1980, Olympic gold. Annemarie invested in the Café Annemarie at her home village of Kleinarl, married one of Rohrmoser's ski representatives, Herbert Moser, and set the six crystal globes awarded for her World Cup titles in a public showcase. While she went out to conquer the world, Herbert sold World Cup T shirts and signed postcards of his wife together with the Vienna coffee and pastries. Annemarie's flat features, pale blue eyes and hair saved from mousiness by a tinge of celtic red may not offer conventional glamour; her figure is hour-glass in coiled hawser. Her immediate celebration after a race was a puff on a tipped cigarette. But when she retired just before the 1976 Winter Olympics in Innsbruck, Austria reeled. Partly, it was said, it was because Rohrmoser was too stingy. But, after quietly nursing her dying father, herself undergoing a stomach operation, watching the bills mount at the café, and reckoning herself too young to give up, she made a comeback at twenty-six.

Then came the snag and the typical fudging of modern ski-racing. During her retirement she had earned $7750 from a television commercial which showed her

Annemarie Moser-Proell: six times World Cup winner who made a ski famous

triumphing over, not a downhill course, but a nasty-looking jelly stain. Since Annemarie's main object in returning was to win her first Olympic gold medal – Marie-Therese Nadig twice foiled her by hundredths of a second in Sapporo in 1972 – it required the Austrian Olympic Committee to assure the IOC categorically that she had paid over the fee to them. She won her gold, overcoming quite a serious training injury, and Herbert was able to tell the world, 'Now she stay at home and get children.'

Manufacturers pay out large sums to underwrite amateur ski-racing. In all, a world star in 1982 might expect contracts worth up to $300,000 (or £150,000). The annual racing budget of a leading ski-maker would be about £500,000. Development and other buried costs make it much higher, although recession has caused some cutbacks. Each top racer may be featured in advertisements provided the manufacturer pays money to the national pool. The manufacturers have advertisement writers on permanent standby to blast out copy immediately a contracted racer wins on their product.

But a win it has to be. There are huge differences between, say, the Mahre twins and most others in the US ski team. The ski manufacturer, K2, may put around $120,000 into the US team on account of Phil and Steve exclusively using their product. They are permitted to advertise themselves as official suppliers and to use the twins promotionally. The twins will be paid via funding from the US Educational Ski Foundation which obviously must take account of their prowess,

success, expenses and future needs. K2 sell about 120,000 pairs of skis annually in the USA, so of every pair sold one dollar may be marked down to the Mahre twins. An 18-year-old newcomer, gamely making it through the ruts on to the US team, is, in almost every sense, an amateur and has to be supported as such. The Swiss Federation, more open than some Alpine countries, pay fixed sums for World Cup success – $7000 for a win and $45,000 for an overall World Cup victory. With various perks, a World Cup downhill win is worth about $50,000.

Many skiers dislike the hypocrisy of the 'amateur' circuit and in recent seasons Ingemar Stenmark and the two Wenzels, Hanni and Andreas, joint World Cup winners in 1979–80, have taken out so-called 'B' licences, which enable them to keep their endorsement profits to themselves but precludes them ever again skiing an Olympics. It was a system first worked out by the Swiss and Heini Hemmi, a veteran who needed to cash in quickly after winning the Innsbruck Olympics giant slalom. Curiously, FIS have no exact regulations covering a B licence. A sport so conditioned to 'force majeure' on the mountainside – in other words circumstances which can overwhelm known procedures – finds itself able to make many accommodations. The British campaigned a long time for open skiing. When it arrived it did so by a convenient back door.

The endless fudging of the World Cup scoring system has been another example of multi-national and commercial pressures at work. There has scarcely been a year since 1967 when there has been no major or minor amendment. In the seventies it was ostensibly to encourage the all-rounder. Specifically it was to stop an individual – first Gustavo Thoeni, then Ingemar Stenmark – from winning year after year because they were outstandingly the best giant and special slalomers. The World Cup committee tried going back to the original 1967 formula of all races counting, and Stenmark still won because there were so many more races. They tried limiting scoring to only the best four races in each discipline and giving points down to the twenty-fifth finisher instead of the first ten. In 1978–9 Peter Luescher of Switzerland was the most embarrassed winner of all time: a goodish slalomer and giant slalomer, he only won one race and never made the top twenty-five to score a point in downhill. He simply entered downhill to score points in the combined in what Stenmark dismisses as 'paper races', a set of marks for those who enter both downhill and slalom at certain nominated events. Poor Luescher has gone down in history as Peter Loser, but his name remains on the World Cup scroll.

This season, less controversially, the racers can again count their best five results in each discipline, scoring is for the top fifteen only (25 for first, 20 for second, then 15, 12, 11, 10, etc., down to 1 for fifteenth), and a maximum of three combined results can be counted (without them Phil Mahre could not have won the 1981 World Cup). But with a smaller programme because of the World Championships at Schladming the World Cup is set for the familiar turbulence.

2

SKI SUNDAY AND TELEVISION

David Vine

I suppose we knew it had worked when one morning, ploughing through the post, I opened a letter addressed to David Vine, The Ski Man on Sundays, BBC Television, London. The writing on the envelope conjured up a picture of an inky ball-pen clasped between stubby little fingers, the writer's tongue sticking out between his lips and tracing every word. I don't think I was far out because the letter inside said, quite simply: 'Dear Sir, Can you please tell me who was thirteenth in the giant slalom race three weeks ago as I have missed his world cup points off my chart. Thank you . . .', and it was signed by a twelve-year-old in Birmingham. I almost wrote back and asked him if I could borrow his chart because the over-complicated points system of the World Cup gives everyone nightmares. Commentators and journalists spend more than a moment or two checking each other's charts.

But, as I say, we knew the gamble of 'Ski Sunday' had worked if we'd managed to obtain that sort of interest with a sport where there are no Kevin Keegans or Ian Bothams for the British fans to hero-worship. Instead we had to try and get them worshipping a dour Swede who makes news when he actually says something revolutionary like 'Perhaps'! We had to get the casual Sunday afternoon TV fan to watch – and keep watching – people he'd never heard of and whose faces he couldn't see coming one after another down a snow-covered mountain. He'd probably never heard of the mountain either!

BBC Television, of course, had always covered the winter sports but only in any kind of detail when it came to the Olympic Games. Ski Jumping caught the imagination of the British public in terms of spectacle but one man was responsible for the 'gamble' of a regular Sunday series on Alpine ski-racing. That man was Franz Klammer, an Austrian farmer's son who, in the Winter Olympic Games of 1976, raced down the side of a mountain outside Innsbruck in a way the world had never seen before. Klammer broke every rule in the ski book. Every second we all said: 'He's gone'. But he hadn't – and he went on and on, arms waving like a windmill, leaping and jumping until he finally reached the bottom. Klammer

Above: Franz Klammer created a new viewing public. *Opposite top:* 'Swing with him . . . zoom in.' The cameras provide a continuous pictorial strip, the commentator in his tiny box a verbal back-up, identifying, informing, interpreting the flickering figures. *Opposite below:* Interviewing is part of the job. Austrian TV talks with Peter Wirnsberger, while (*left to right*) Peter Mueller, Steve Podborski (the winner) and Harti Weirather wait

had gone faster than anyone and he was the most spectacular Olympic champion ever. My colleague, Ron Pickering, who was the Alpine commentator at those Games, was as excited as anyone. 'The crowd are going wild . . . balloons are going up!' Well, the balloon went up shortly after that and we launched 'Ski Sunday'.

   This coming season is our biggest yet, incorporating the World Championships at Schladming, Austria, where just about everyone who really moves on skis will be on the screen. So how does it all work? More than once I ask myself that! Usually on a Thursday I fly out of Heathrow with a producer and, after a combination of aeroplanes, trains, cars and mountain railways, with any luck – and anyone who's travelled the snow show will know about that – we arrive at our hotel. It's probably full, some continental office has got the booking wrong, and so it takes a lot of talking before you get a bed. The place is already packed with racers, back-up teams and the inevitable camp followers – they're the ones with the fantastic sun tans, long blonde hair and the very latest fashion in ski wear, before and après. For us, it's a quick unpack, on with the long johns and down to the race office to find out what there is to find out. I talk with ski managers and racers, the producer talks with the foreign TV company who will be responsible for providing the pictures. After a day of practice and a day and half a night

getting record cards up to date, we're on the hill – or at least trying to squeeze into a telephone booth laughingly called a commentary box.

Surrounding us are ski commentators from all over the world – and like us they're shouting down microphones trying to make contact with their TV centres back home. It's like a United Nations riot. Somehow, every piece of wire is eventually plugged into the right hole, after a few nightmare moments when I realise I have been having a fascinating conversation with a TV Producer in Yugoslavia! In your headphones, you hear a voice in broken English (God bless what is supposed to be one of the international Eurovision languages) saying 'Stand by'. And then you're on, relying completely on the pictures the foreign director gives you, the pictures you're seeing back home beside the fire. Out of the commentary box window you can see only the last hundred metres or so of the downhill track, which is why you've been up the mountain the day before studying the course. It's now your job to interpret the mass of timing figures that appear on the screen, identify the racer, describe his performance, and finally get the result right.

Back in Television Centre in London, a small army of people are working on the incoming mixture of foreign pictures and your voice – and gradually the whole thing comes together, ending perhaps with an interview I've managed to get with the star of the day, and beginning with that montage of ski action and music which is now an established part of BBC Television's sports coverage. And that's all there is to it . . . almost.

After another race on the Sunday, we're hotfooting out of the resort, getting back into London on Monday with just Tuesday and perhaps Wednesday to sort out the next one, check the programme everyone watched at home, squeeze in a few other matters and then off again. That's December, January and February for the 'Ski Sunday' team.

This season, for the World Championships which only come around once every four years, we'll be camping out for a fortnight in Schladming and Haus, twin Austrian resorts south of Salzburg, and then straight on to the next World Cup venue. The racers are people we eat with and we're lucky enough to have the chance of the odd evening around a log fire – or a video screen – finding out what makes them take part in this fascinating and at times terrifying sport. And make no mistake, the moments we all dread come far too often.

Last season was an exceptional one when it came to survival. No one had ever seen so many experts in the business flying through the air like rag dolls and crashing into straw bales, nylon nets and spectators – and no one will ever forget the sight of Switzerland's Peter Mueller, only metres from the finish line on the Lauberhorn at Wengen, suddenly losing control. One moment, the big blond champion was every inch a winner. In a hundredth of a second he was a horrifying bundle of arms, legs, skis and sticks, chopping through the barriers and the crowd like the blades of a helicopter. I know I leapt out of the chair on which I was perched – and I could see it all through the window as well as on the screen – and

changed my words from 'And Mueller has won' to 'And Mueller has gone'. It was probably more of a scream than a commentary. I was petrified. Within a second the next racer was in view at the top of the mountain. It was quite a long time before I was able to say that Mueller, who'd crashed at over 80 mph, seemed to have nothing more wrong with him than a cracked shoulder. A few weeks later he was standing beside me at another World Cup venue and had already been on skis again.

Perhaps the man who put it all into perspective was one of the most outrageous characters the 'White Circus' is lucky enough to have. His official occupation is 'chimney sweep', he rarely shaves, has a waistline which pays tribute to his love of the good life, but he has been, and still is, one of the world's great downhill racers. He's an Austrian called Werner Grissman or, as the name on his race helmet spells out, 'Grizzly'. Only last season Grizzly – who these days runs out of steam a little after the half-way mark – was in trouble (again) with his nation's authorities. In a practice race he appeared at the finish and was immediately approached by an Austrian camera crew, complete with interviewer. 'Tell me,' said Austria's David Vine to Grizzly, 'you went very well today on the bottom half of the hill. Have you discovered something which helps you to keep the speed going?' 'Yes,' replied Grizzly, the round, tanned face breaking into the suspicion of a smile. He turned his back to the camera – and strapped onto his ski suit were a couple of firework rockets. Grizzly spent the last 100 metres of a practice run trying to set them alight just to prove he was capable of a jet finish. He was suspended for a little time but apparently he'd committed another 'crime' as well over a boot contract.

But this is a man who can put it all into perspective. When I spoke to him about the danger and the controversy concerning courses that are becoming too fast, he said: 'The courses must be safe, or as safe as they can be made. But don't take away the danger. We live on danger, and without it we have no fun.' Without men like Werner Grissman, or his fellow Austrian Harti Weirather and Steve Podborski of Canada, who are providing the new excitement these days, men like Ingemar Stenmark of Sweden, who says little and with his technical perfection doesn't have to, and men like Konrad Bartelski of Great Britain who has kept the Union Jack flying as high as it's ever been in men's ski-racing, we wouldn't have the danger and the fun that is 'Ski Sunday'.

3

THE WORLD CUP BATTLE
Phil Mahre and Ingemar Stenmark

John Samuel

Phil Mahre is a plain man from America's mountainous north-west, perhaps the one major burden in life that of being a hero. Luckily he has a fraternal twin, Steve, who finished fourth overall, and as misty-eyed Americans waved the Stars and Stripes in the little Swiss village of Laax on 27 March, the back that was slapped on that famous day in ski-racing as often as not was Steve's as Phil's. Steve is an inch taller, a little less round, has a small bump on the back of his head and they are not identical in the strict biological sense, but to the world they are identical and Steve's share in events was a part of the triumph of the occasion.

The day was famous for many reasons. Mahre was the first English-speaking winner of the men's World Cup overall title. In the end a series straddling thirty-one events, three continents and 30,000 miles of travelling, had come down to a blow for blow between two men, Mahre and Ingemar Stenmark. In the final race of the season, a giant slalom, Mahre needed third place to lead Stenmark for the first and only time in a contest which had begun four months earlier. On the end of a second giant slalom run of under ninety seconds was the World Cup and the knowledge, given to few at the age of twenty-four, that he would never again in his life have to worry seriously about money.

Like the downhill finish between Harti Weirather and Steve Podborski at Aspen three weeks earlier, it had the classic ingredients of a final between men of contrasts and similarities, enormously respectful of each other, preserving their courtesies and mountain reticence through all the hubbub. On the one hand Stenmark, the finest technical skier of all time, native of Tarnaby in Sweden – a few clapboard houses and barely a main street – close to the Arctic circle and the Norwegian border in the heart of Scandinavia. On the other Mahre, native of White Pass, Washington, population 27, whose father, Dave, area ski manager and climber of every mountain in the north-west, taught his nine children simple things. 'The body will always be a quitter, the body will lie down. The Bible doesn't lie when it says faith – the mind, whatever you want to call it – can move mountains.'

Left: Phil Mahre, first English-speaking winner of the men's World Cup. *Below:* Twin brother Steve, four minutes older, took fourth place overall. Continentals were astonished when he checked his brother at Borovetz. *Bottom:* Phil Mahre: an overtake on the finish line was part of America's game plan

Stenmark, 25, winner of two Olympic and two World Championship golds and three World Cup titles (in 1976/7/8) – a total of sixty-two major victories and 100 top-ten finishes in 126 starts. Mahre, 24, eleven World Cup victories, Olympic slalom silver medallist, feet blistered from playing too much basketball in training, a dozen major and minor leg and ankle bones grafted together from fractures in 1973, 1974 and 1979. The first accident was in an avalanche at White Pass, the second in training, the third in the Lake Placid pre-Olympics giant slalom. Phil skied the early part of the Olympic season with a battery built into his boot which warmed the plate and screws of his rehabilitating ankle.

In World Cup overall Mahre finished second in 1978 to Stenmark, third in 1979 to Peter Luescher, his injury almost certainly costing him the title, and third in 1980 to Andreas Wenzel. At the end of the 1979–80 season he came close to quitting. Racing had lost some of its savour. It was a sum of many things: the unremitting grind of the circuit, the gypsy nature of the living for teams from outside the continent of Europe, a broken marriage and a latent feeling, perhaps, that life might hold a deeper commitment than ski-racing. Against it was unfulfilled ambition, the desire once and for all to explode the Mr Runner-up syndrome so detestable to Americans, but one which strongly attached to their men skiers. No American male had ever won a major Alpine ski title.

So Mahre took the summer off, with lots of water-skiing, and came back in the autumn with spirits renewed. At Killington, Vermont, he worked on building strength, making good turns and skiing aggressively. 'I'm concentrating on skiing down the hill instead of across it or up it,' he said. Already by then Mahre and the US chief coach, Konrad Rickenbach, Swiss-born but living in California since he was a child, had prepared a game plan. Mahre finds downhill a bore. 'I've always been relaxed skiing downhill. But in GS [giant slalom] there are always different courses and lots of variation. In downhill, after three days training on the same course, you find the race a real bore. I'm not saying anything against downhillers, it's just not me for preference.' But he and Rickenbach knew that he had to ski up to five downhills to qualify for the combined points which could take the World Cup globe to the US for the first time. The combined, contemptuously dismissed by Stenmark as a 'paper' race, is a bonus set of marks, the usual 25 for first place and so on down to fifteenth place, for results in downhill twinned with a slalom or GS. Five twin events are nominated in the calendar, from which a racer in 1980–1 could count his best three. The US Think Tank knew that if Phil Mahre could spring the maximum 75 points from combined, he would need precisely 176 points on the snow to defeat Stenmark, assuming the Swede kept to his vow of never skiing downhill. Stenmark could reliably be expected to win five giant slalom (he was unbeaten in this discipline for nearly two years up to Waterville in March 1980) and five giant slaloms, making 250 points for the season. Mahre needed 251 to win. But the game plan went just a little astray . . .

Mahre's start was less than encouraging – a postponed GS at Val d'Isère and forty-fifth place in a downhill that just survived the blizzard. Stenmark came

winging into the circuit with victories in the slalom and GS of Madonna di Campiglio and the pattern of the campaign was set – the Swede racking up a mountain of points and Mahre left to pursue him hand over hand up the face. On 31 December, after four downhills, one slalom, two giant slaloms and two combineds, Stenmark was close behind Peter Mueller, a downhill specialist, overall, and Phil Mahre thirty-seventh. Slowly the gap narrowed. Steve Mahre won his first World Cup race since 1978 at Garmisch-Partenkirchen, West Germany, on 11 January, and Phil, not to be outdone, gained his best-ever downhill finish of thirteenth. While Ken Read was bombing out to ruin one set of North American hopes in downhill, Phil was adding his first bonus of 25 combined points, coupling up his fourth place in the Morzine GS. It was an important occasion for the Americans, Phil's victory a proof that they were on the right lines. But another twist to the plot was in the making. Postponements due to lack of snow were making the scheduled twinning impossible, and *ad hoc* decisions from week to week decided which downhill went with what slalom for a combined. Stenmark was keeping a closer than usual eye on it, and already his Italian adviser, Hermann Nogler, was doing his arithmetic.

Stenmark would not be safe on 250 points. At the last moment, so late that it provoked an unsuccessful US protest, he entered for the Kitzbuehel downhill in pursuit of combined points to go with his second place in the Oberstaufen slalom four days previously. The twinning was in such confusion that the Kitzbuehel slalom was not paired with the Kitzbuehel downhill, but as ever in ski-racing, some bright minds were knitting plain and purl and not getting in a tangle. Stenmark, stooped uncomfortably in a skintight suit, descended the mighty Streif ten seconds behind the winner in thirty-fourth place, but good enough for a third place in combined and 15 points to stretch Mahre's theoretical target to 266 points. Stenmark now topped the overall with 150 points and from here on the downhillers faded out of the overall campaign. 'If you want to race downhill you cannot train for slalom,' Stenmark said. 'And vice versa.'

Downhill, as he was prepared to admit, does give him fear. He suffered severe concussion the previous season in secret downhill practice on the glacier at Val Senales. 'It wasn't a difficult course, but it included a compression – a dip and a rise after a steep section. We don't experience that in slalom. I entered the compression too far back on my skis. The course went one way and I went the other.' With this experience it was more than ever courageous to tackle Kitzbuehel. Phil Mahre's challenge had scarcely started to ripen; even so, it proved a far-sighted decision. Stenmark won the Adelboden GS with Mahre slipping to eighth, but as the clouds parted at St Anton for the Arlberg–Kandahar, the American eagle unfurled its wings over this silvery sunlit scene.

St Anton has long held English-speaking associations. The Arlberg–Kandahar itself is the oldest Alpine race, a pioneering venture by the Austrian Hannes Schneider and the Englishman Arnold Lunn, who put a high price on all-round ability. In the Bahnhof bar, where a motley of Americans, British, Canadians and

Ingemar Stenmark: seeking a fourth World Cup victory in his first year as a professional

South Africans meet regularly and even produce their own newspaper, the *Bugel*, there was cause for celebration on 1 February. Stenmark had won the slalom, but only twelve hundredths behind was Mahre, and twentieth place in downhill gave him his third and final 25-point award in the combineds. 'My time is coming,' he said. 'I always ski better in February and March, and we have races soon in the US.' Stenmark 200 points, Mahre 168. All the combineds gone, everything now to play for on the snow.

Neither Stenmark nor Mahre admits to any other policy than taking each race as it comes, never consciously saying, 'This is important for the World Cup. This I must do in this time or that.' Stenmark claims no special physical aptitudes, but then nor does Bjorn Borg. He is a remarkable standing jumper, but, with all his training, what else? Or so he will say. Stenmark does concede that to win he must get angry. It eliminates unproductive nervousness. He can psych himself up, getting annoyed by what someone has said, or what he has read. Never by thinking he is skiing for Sweden, much as his countrymen and women dote on him. 'I do not ski for my country, I ski for myself,' he says. 'And after a few gates there is no anger, only concentration on the course.' At the finish he stands quietly surveying the scene, unfailingly courteous to other racers, his diffidence observed and respected by all who would seek to lionise him.

In Schladming Mahre stuttered. Stenmark won the rescheduled GS with the American sixth. Rickenbach assessed the final legs. Stenmark on home snow

The final race: Phil Mahre zooms to second place, Stenmark is third. The US are triumphant

in Scandinavia, and the run-in via Aspen, Furano (Japan), Borovetz (Bulgaria), with the last race due in Kranjska Gora (Yugoslavia). 'Phil won't ski the two Aspen downhills. We're concentrating wholly on the four giant slaloms and five specials. We need seven places in the top three in the nine remaining races and Phil can win.' He did not quite achieve it. Mahre placed top three in six of them, but three of these were victories and in two other races he was fourth. It was, however, enough. Mahre's victory in the slalom at Are (Sweden), where Stenmark had never lost, was his first since Jasna in 1979. Psychologically it was a dagger thrust. The tired Swede could score no more GS points and only raced in Aspen to try and stop Mahre scoring more. He wanted to take a break in Hawaii and prepare for Furano, but his coach, Jean-Pierre Chatellard, urged him to try and block the American. After the long journey into the enemy's lair Mahre was first, Stenmark second. The effort had been in vain. Stenmark 260 points, Mahre 234 and five events remaining.

Mahre kept up the heat. In the Furano slalom it was Mahre first, Stenmark second again. 'I am tired of racing,' the Swede declared. 'I have no more motivation for the first runs where I lose too much ground.' Stenmark is famous for his comebacks from seemingly impossible situations. He was reaching down and finding plenty still, but not enough to catch Mahre. At Borovetz Mahre at last suffered a check – from his brother. The European press could hardly believe it. Stenmark had fallen; Phil was all set for second place behind the Russian,

Celebration postponed: Phil has work to do after his World Cup-winning run. Instructions to brother Steve

Alexander Zhirov, when along came Steve to push him into third place. A potential gain of 8 points is only 3 . . . and the opportunity to win the World Cup there and then was gone.

So to the final race, which had been switched to Laax because of thin snow in Kransjka Gora, and Mahre must be third or better in the final race, a giant slalom. Eleven days into spring the morning is fine. Both GS runs are scheduled for the same day. The agony will not be prolonged. Mahre is unshaven, Stenmark all in white. They are alone together. Everyone respects their need for concentration. Mahre throws himself down the course like a quarter-back going for the line – 1 minute 20.79 seconds. Stenmark is just ahead, by three hundredths of a second. The snow is getting warmer in the hot sun. Mahre is well used to soft snow in the Cascades. The icier the course the better Stenmark likes it. Suddenly the wind blows from the east – Zhirov, Russian winner of four of the last five slalom and giant slalom races, hurtles down in 1:18.75 for an overall 2:39.80. Starting next, Mahre cannot beat it, but 1:19.26 for 2:40.05 looks good. So it is. Stenmark manages only 1:19.48 and is third. It's over. Phil Mahre is the World Cup overall

Time to stand and stare: fatigue and disappointment show in Stenmark's face as he watches the celebrations around Mahre

champion, but before the CBS television commentator, Billy Kidd, can interview him, Phil is grabbing a walkie-talkie to the top. Steve must be briefed.

'Get the rhythm at the start, get around that first pitch. Make good crisp turns, then on the sidehill below work towards that last little pitch. After that let 'em run. Nail that last little turn for the last flat down there.' As often as not all season, it has been Steve filling in Phil. His advice in Are, where Stenmark was beaten on home snow, was crucial. 'It was as if I'd raced it myself,' said Phil. Stenmark was the first to congratulate him, then stayed around, bravely fielding the runner-up questions.

Phil Mahre went home to build a house in the fifty acres of choice land he owns in Eastern Washington. Pounding nails is as much a part of Phil Mahre the man as Phil Mahre the skier. 'I've learned how to be both a winner and a loser,' he says. 'It's a very healthy atmosphere. It gives you the desire not to rush things in life. Right now there's a very good chance I'll be at Sarajevo [the 1984 Olympics], but a lot of things can happen in three years, including the possibility of injury. But as long as I enjoy the sport I'll do it whether it's one year or ten.'

4

THE DOWNHILL BATTLE
Harti Weirather and Steve Podborski

Matt Fisher

The favourites at the start of the 1980–1 World Cup downhill season were clear-cut – Switzerland's Peter Mueller, 23, champion in the two previous seasons, and Canada's Ken Read, 25, another in his downhill prime, winner at Kitzbuehel and Wengen the previous season. The one from Zurich, the other from Calgary – city men, from a competitive background, with ready access to mountains. In December 1980 there were no bets that a deceptively lean and lightly regarded farmer's son from the Austrian Tyrol would be the next champion of the World Cup's glamour event. Nor did anyone think that the farmer's son, Harti Weirather, would have to beat another relative unknown, Canadian Steve Podborski, on the last day of the season, to claim the title and millions of Austrian schillings.

Austria expected, even demanded, results. They had won forty-eight of the 102 World Cup downhills to the beginning of 1980–1 but the last two titles had gone to their arch rival, Switzerland. There had been serious Swiss challenges to Austrian downhill supremacy before, from Roland Collombin and Bernhard Russi, but Franz Klammer had put paid to that streak, winning twenty-two races between 1974 and 1978. Who now would put away Mueller and Read?

Weirather's roommate and good friend Peter Wirnsberger was tipped to lead the Austrian team back to glory with an assortment of others, including Olympic champion Leonhard Stock, former champion Klammer, and the autumn training leader, Uli Spiess, rated as outside chances. That Weirather was seldom mentioned was not surprising. He had quietly advanced to the first seed during the 1979–80 season but he had never won a race. His second places at Kitzbuehel and Lake Louise were strong indications of future possibilities but the Austrian press preferred to concentrate on the boyishly good-looking Wirnsberger, the thoughtful and eloquent Spiess and the playful antics of bad boy Werner Grissman, who often receives more ink for his après-ski accomplishments than for his achievements on the hill. Whichever post-race party to be honoured with the presence of the self-styled 'Grizzly' was sure to generate the most noise and a mention in the next day's tabloids. He had not won since 1972.

Harti Weirather: no bets that he could be downhill champion at the start of 1980–1

It was against this backdrop that the shy and unfailingly polite Weirather began his ascent to the top of the downhill world in December 1980 with a first and a second in the double downhill at Val Gardena, the Romanish and German-speaking town in the Italian Tyrol. A week before, at 'the Criterium of the First Snow' at Val d'Isère, Spiess triumphed, finishing ahead of four Canadians. Recently married, and twenty pounds lighter than ever before, he was quickly adopted as Austria's new hope. Even in a non-winning capacity at Val Gardena he maintained his fame by turning the Camel bumps from a triple into a double. His season and possibly his career ended with a thud on 19 December at St Moritz when he attempted another spectacular pre-jump in training.

Spiess's tumble (torn knee ligaments, broken ribs, concussion) was the first in a series which eventually stripped away more than a quarter of the favoured first seed. Olympic downhill champion Leonhard Stock's much-admired technical abilities did him little good at Garmisch where he spun out of control and into a snow fence with broken vertebrae. Further down the same course Ken Read caught an edge only metres from a probable second-place finish. His left ski stayed on as his body wound down from 80 mph. When he finally stopped he had facial cuts, a broken nose and, worst of all, torn knee ligaments.

The victims: *left to right*, Ken Read tore knee ligaments; Peter Mueller dislocated a shoulder;

While others were crashing, Podborski astounded the ski world by putting together consecutive victories at St Moritz, Garmisch and Kitzbuehel. It was a remarkable achievement for a skier who had only one pre-season goal: to remain in the first seed. Podborski had torn ligaments in his right knee for the second time while free skiing in Austria the previous May; his summer was spent in a cast. As he could not run on the leg when the cast came off a weightlifting and cycling programme was devised: 1000 hours were spent bringing the knee around. The first on-snow test came in October and the first race training was attempted only five days before the first race at Val d'Isère, where he was third. Although Podborski was still unable to run, the knee had withstood 'G' forces ten times his body weight.

With Read, Stock and Spiess out of the running, Podborski had become the odds-on favourite to win North America its first downhill title. After Kitzbuehel, Weirather and Mueller, who had won the other race at Val Gardena, were the only skiers with a chance to catch the happy-go-lucky Canadian with the diamond stud in his left ear. Perhaps worried by Podborski's tremendous race results after lack-lustre training times ('Why should I risk the knee?'), Mueller came flying out of the final turn at Wengen, a week later, fully half a second ahead of the time which Podborski was to record minutes later. If Mueller could hang on, a third title could still, possibly, be his. Unfortunately for him he couldn't. Out of control, having miscalculated the turn, he slammed into a stack of frozen hay bales only metres from certain victory. A dislocated shoulder put him out for six long weeks. Another Swiss, Toni Buergler, was first, Weirather second and Podborski third.

On the following Saturday, at St Anton, Buergler crashed after posting the best

Leonhard Stock broke vertebrae; and Uli Spiess broke ribs, tore knee ligaments and was concussed

section time and Weirather, skiing 'my best race of the season', was first. Podborski was once again third and Weirather was finally equal with him in points. The ski circus then packed its bags and headed down the road to Schladming. The race was to be held on the Planai, site of the 1982 World Championships, a high-speed course known to some as an 'autobahn' but to most as 'the Canadian downhill' because only Canadians have won there since 1975. Podborski had been the latest to honour that tradition, recording the best time by more than a second before rain forced the cancellation of a race in December 1979.

Rain once again forced the abandonment of the 1981 Schladming downhill, but not before 600 journalists had filed mountains of copy on Weirather and Podborski, scrutinising their rather slow training times, their profound respect for each other, and the considerable differences between their national teams. Austria was and still is the world's premier downhill nation but the Canadian challenge has grown stronger by the year. In 1975 the 'Crazy Canucks' or 'Kamikaze Canadians' were born with the surprise victories of Read and Dave Irwin. After a number of spectacular crashes slowed Irwin down, Read became the team's leader, scoring occasional victories in 1978 and 1979. In 1980 he won the coveted Kitzbuehel–Wengen double. Meanwhile Podborski, who didn't really fit the 'Crazy Canuck' image because of his much more controlled skiing style, was slowly accumulating a string of seconds and thirds. His only victory came at Morzine in 1978, when Read was disqualified for wearing an illegal suit.

The Canadian team's first mentor was Scott Henderson, a laconic Albertan who moved the team towards downhill specialisation before leaving in 1977 after a dispute with Read and others over training tactics. His replacement was another

Steve Podborski: just one more victory, but it kept eluding him

quiet Westerner, John Ritchie. Because of limited funds and a small group of skiers to choose from, Ritchie runs one of the smallest teams on the World Cup. It consists of four 'A' team racers, two coaches, a masseur, a video man, a doctor, and one or two service representatives who are paid by European manufacturers.

The Canadian team does not look like much beside the Austrian team, with its full complement of ten downhill racers and a support staff of about twenty. The Austrians get additional back-up from a large pool of ski manufacturers and from huge provincial and club programmes. However, in spite of these considerable resources there has been little to choose between the two countries' best in the last few years. 'The difference is that they have a few more people to help with things like timing,' explains Heinz Kappeler, who joined the Canadian team four years ago after working with the Swiss 'B' team. 'Having a horde of service people doesn't always help you. The Austrians have so many that they have trouble keeping them away from the team. They try to influence the racers behind the coaches' backs. It puts the athletes in a difficult position.' Perhaps Canada's biggest advantage is that its small group has been a homogeneous unit since 1977. During the same period of time the Austrians have had many staff changes. 'Continuity is very important,' says Kappeler. 'Everyone knows what to do, especially on race day. We're well organised and don't waste much time.'

When the Weirather–Podborski duel resumed a month later in Aspen, Colorado, only a handful of journalists were in attendance. And because no American

television network had bought rights to what had become (because of the Schladming wash-out) a double downhill, the Austrian network, ORF, could not send the race home. Canada's CBC made do with a film report of the race.

To everyone's surprise Valeri Tsyganov, of the Soviet Union, won the first race. The skier from the Arctic Kola peninsula had given Russia its first downhill victory ever in the World Cup. Weirather was second and Podborski tenth, having made a critical mistake on the Aztec turn near the top. Weirather moved into the World Cup downhill lead by five points. The decisive race would take place on the same course twenty-four hours later.

Podborski drew number one, Weirather fourteen. Correcting his error on the Aztec Podborski improved on Weirather's previous day's time and began the long wait to see whether Weirather could do even better and take the title. Podborski had to finish first or second, with Weirather third or worse. One possible stumbling block was removed when Tsyganov crashed; another disappeared when Peter Mueller, back after his shoulder injury, had a poor run.

Word of Podborski's time, and the slow times of other racers, was relayed to an anxious Weirather by radio. He was behind Podborski at both the first and second time points, but flashed across the finish line four hundredths of a second ahead. 'I knew I had a chance', he explained moments later, 'because I was out of control many times. I made the many little mistakes you make when you are going as fast as you can.' Could Hollywood have arranged it better?

Weirather's victory was greeted with relief by Austrians, who had grown fat on the twenty-two victories Franz Klammer put together during the mid-seventies. Mueller's two titles and the occasional Canadian victory were treated as aberrations, an interregnum between Austrian champions. Except for Weirather's great success they had had a grey season. Only one other downhill (Spiess at Val d'Isère) was won by an Austrian.

Weirather is acutely aware of the responsibilities of an Austrian racer. He says, 'When you lose, Austrians think *they* have lost. It means lots of business for our ski manufacturers and helps attract visitors who come to ski. For example, tourism should be better in my village, Reutte, which lies on the German frontier. The Germans are keen skiers and may want to ski where I ski.'

During Weirather's three-month race to the top of the downhill World Cup he had had doubts about whether he had a chance to be the next champion. He recalls, 'I really didn't think I had any chance at all until after my first victory at Val Gardena. Then Podborski won the next three races. After that I knew my chances of winning were not great but not impossible. Of course if I hadn't won at Aspen I wouldn't have been champion, but for me the key was my good showing at Wengen, followed by my win at St Anton. At Kitzbuehel [where Podborski had won his third straight race] I had been fifth. At Wengen I was second and it gave me a lot of confidence. By the time I got to Aspen I knew I could win.'

Such public confessions do not come easily to Weirather. Although something of a practical joker with friends he prefers the safety of large groups or anonymous

hotel rooms where he can concentrate on the race at hand or read a favourite detective story. His interest in mysteries and science fiction set him somewhat apart from his rowdier teammates who prefer shooting pool or playing cards in their spare time. Like many of them he attended the prestigious 'Ski Gymnasium' at Stams, thirty kilometres west of Innsbruck, combining orthodox studies with ski school.

He follows what he calls 'a regular routine'. It includes the usual Austrian dry-land programme – cycling, soccer, volleyball, basketball, mountain hiking, and gymnastics like the rings, horizontal bar and trampoline. In addition he takes an occasional turn on his father's farm, helping cut wood and manage sixty dairy cows and 100 pigs. He and a younger brother, who doesn't ski-race, help most when the summer's two crops of hay have to be brought in. Klammer and Stock are two other racers who come from farming families.

Weirather's hobbies, motorcross racing and water-skiing, also help keep him in shape. He is also an accomplished marksman 'but I don't like to kill things . . . I like to look at nature'. With the arguable exception of Hans Enn, Weirather is considered to be the Austrian team's finest athlete. In street clothes he looks slight. Only in a downhill or bathing suit can you see the large legs and back muscles which take him down mountains at speeds of up to 80 mph or more.

Weirather has been described by teammates in the competitive Austrian racing environment as 'a truly nice guy. He has good relations with everyone.' Those good relations apparently even extend to head coach Charlie Kahr, who is not known for getting along with his racers. But even the affable Weirather had one misunderstanding with Kahr. According to Austrian newspaper reports, Weirather 'tricked' Kahr into giving him extra training by telling him that he wanted to become a combined (downhill–slalom) skier like the Olympic hero, Leonhard Stock. What Weirather apparently wanted was to get the giant slalom training he felt he needed to prepare for the downhill season. He got seven to ten extra days of training in October, with a higher GS to downhill training ratio than any of his downhill teammates. Later, the training finished, Weirather informed Kahr that he had no intention of skiing anything but downhill. What is said to have upset Kahr is that the media got hold of the story. Weirather's victories certainly healed whatever rift there was.

'The extra training helped a lot,' says Weirather, 'because I improved my turns and learned better how to position myself to win races. In the downhill you almost always have to use a downhill turn. Training giant slalom just gives you a better feeling for the turns when they come. You can improve your time and weight transfer. It is important to work on the turns because it is difficult. Skiing straight is no problem.'

Looking ahead to the current season, Weirather predicted that it would be very difficult for him to remain as champion. 'I hope to have two or three victories but there will be more competition,' he said. 'Podborski will be back and he is a superman. The only difference between us last year was that I had luck. It was

Off-duty downhiller: Weirather's slight appearance is deceptive. Leg and back muscles are of the 90-mph man

such a close competition. Ken Read will be back, too, and he is a great man in skiing. So is Uli [Spiess] who would have been good last year if he hadn't been hurt. Peter Mueller should also have regained his health. Then there are the new stars like Franz Heinzer [of Switzerland] and Gerhard Pfaffenbichler [of Austria] who are going to be much better. I think that what you're going to see is a new generation of downhill racers with much better technique than in the past. Klammer used to win without getting the turns and jumps right. Now everything must be as near perfect as possible.'

Weirather is perhaps the best example of the new wave. Although clearly not as exciting as Franz Klammer in his prime – arms flailing like windmills – his smooth technical proficiency and seemingly effortless carved turns have carried him to the bottom of the hill and the top of the downhill world faster than anyone could have imagined.

THE FUTURE OF
WORLD CUP DOWNHILL SKIING
A Racer's View

Ken Read

Ski-racing is a sport in constant change. With the search for speed, the shaving of precious hundredths of seconds from every run, innovation has become the trademark of the sport. New records are being established each year on virtually every course.

What factors have influenced this dramatic change in Alpine skiing? In 1972 we witnessed the last of the all-round skier. Almost simultaneously emerged the specialist in downhill or the technical events (slalom and/or giant slalom). Gone were Killy and Schranz. A new generation of specialists captured the headlines: Thoeni and Gros in the technical disciplines, and Russi, Collombin and the great Franz Klammer in downhill.

Specialisation brought an increasing sophistication of the athlete in his particular discipline. Meeting the competitive demands required super conditioning and extensive ski training. Skiing on glaciers from September to November, with constant refinement of technique, became a necessity for all the top teams. The physical training programme became a full-year commitment, all geared to a four-month competition period from December to April. Total commitment was essential if the goal was to compete successfully with the world's best.

The advance in ski-equipment technology in the mid-seventies was explosive. Suddenly there were sophisticated racing waxes, contour downhill poles, skin-tight aerodynamic downhill suits, and of greatest significance, faster and faster racing skis. In the 1980s specialisation and technology have combined to introduce a new generation of ski-racers with a new approach to the sport. Today's racers are taking it to new levels, refining the final area of change – technique and conditioning. With superior ski equipment and complex training programmes, it now takes a superbly conditioned, highly trained and dedicated athlete to win.

Two distinct approaches to downhill racing have emerged. There is the quiet, smooth, almost passive racer exemplified by Harti Weirather and Steve Podborski. In contrast are the aggressive, all-out attackers typified by Peter Mueller and Peter Wirnsberger. Both approaches have met with success and,

Top: All-out attacker: Olympic silver medallist Peter Wirnsberger
Bottom: Super glider: Switzerland's Peter Mueller, downhill champion of 1979 and 1980

although different, epitomise the physical and technical perfection for which the 'new racer' is striving.

The élite of downhill racing are often viewed as a group of daredevils. In fact they are highly-trained competitors with a keenly developed sense of calculated risk: when and where to push to the limit to shave those extra hundredths of seconds; when to respect the speed and the race course.

But, in the past season, the king of the Alpine disciplines reached a breaking point. An epidemic of injuries occurred, drastically depleting the field of competitors. These injuries were not solely to the inexperienced, less skilled racer. Eight of the top fifteen in the world were struck down, including Olympic champions, world champions and World Cup winners.

Injuries are not happenstance occurrences; they do not occur merely by chance, and are not always the result of racer error. Injuries are not common in World Cup downhill. In fact the injury rate for the recreational skier is higher than for the competitive skier. The most dangerous activity for the downhill racer is in the thousands of miles of automobile travel required to reach competition sites. This sounds absurd, considering the speeds and forces involved in downhill, but statistics show that physical conditioning and snow training serve the competitive skier well.

What then caused the epidemic of last season? It was something that had been building for several years. Technology, training and the search for 'perfection' resulted in the racer challenging the course to the limit. But race courses had not matched the changing times or the World Cup. Course preparation was not adequate to meet the demands of such high speeds. Course-setting did not reflect the changing speeds and acceleration of the skier. Another criticism was that the piste itself was too easy – the so-called autobahn effect – where so many hazards are removed that the course fails to command the racers' respect. Add a few more kilometres per hour and . . . problems!

How then does ski-racing address these problems? What is the challenging, entertaining, but essentially safe downhill of the future? The racers and FIS have got together in the interests of maintaining safety in face of the rapid changes of recent years. FIS now requires an organising committee to hold a Europa Cup downhill the year prior to a World Cup race if the piste has not been used for more than two years. This allows the committee to be more familiar with the course and aware if any changes are needed before the higher-level competition challenges the hill.

This change, along with the formation of a 'piste control group', appointed by FIS to oversee all downhills and recommend any changes, enables a better understanding of each downhill piste and how to correct any problems before a serious injury occurs. To eliminate the 'autobahn effect' FIS has encouraged organisers to retain natural terrain for their downhill courses. This acts as a natural brake. Racers will keep their respect for the hill and speeds will be lower because of the more irregular and thus more difficult terrain to be negotiated.

Crans-Montana, the third stop of the 1981-2 tour, is the first to test this theory with a new 'natural terrain' course.

The approach to the problem is three-pronged. First, to eliminate any surprises in a course due to higher speeds; second, to ensure the safety of the piste; and third, to be more aware of the direction of the sport and how the decisions of today can radically influence the sport of tomorrow.

What will be the downhill of tomorrow? Several changes have been proposed with the object of introducing a more challenging format to the racer, a more interesting competition to the spectator, and a more cost-effective event to the organiser.

The 'Two Day Event' is one proposal. It would involve two days of racing, the first day being a qualification day much like Grand Prix motor-racing. The racer would have to perform on two days, in order to ensure a good start number in qualification for the race on day two. Spectators would then have two days of downhill racing and the organisers two days of high interest in the event and the ski area.

Athlete involvement in the direction of the sport is new and has already had a profound effect. At a meeting in January 1981 the top fifteen downhillers requested several changes. Among these were a minimum of ten downhills a year for the world tour, more races in North America, and the establishment of course and safety standards for all World Cup downhills. FIS responded positively and the 1982 schedule has eleven downhills, with three in North America (at Whistler, Vancouver, and two at Aspen, Colorado). This is now known as the North American tour, and will be an annual section of the World Cup.

FIS encouraged further communication between the athletes and the committees, knowing the purpose of both was to improve the sport and provide an up-to-the-minute point of view of factors influencing it. I was invited to the FIS congress in Tenerife in the spring to comment on problems, especially those affecting safety. Communication has become the policy of the FIS due to the forward-looking attitude of its President, Marc Hodler. He recognises that discussion between athletes, trainers, organisers and administration can contribute to a better sport for all.

Athletes are concerned that the World Cup is more of a world competition than a tour centred in the European Alps. The core of the World Cup will always remain in the Alps, but the success of 'non-alpine' countries such as Canada, Sweden, USA and USSR have stimulated the creation of 'tours'. The Polar World Cup of Scandinavia, the North American tour, and the biennial Japan World Cup are all examples of the emerging internationalism of the World tour. In 1982 the North American tour will be established and 1983 will see the inclusion of the USSR World Cup along with the Japan World Cup.

With greater involvement by different nations, the names of the leaders of the tour have begun to change. The 1980 World Cup in downhill saw the championship disputed between racers from the city of Zurich and the city of Calgary. It is

Breakthrough: Ken Read led the Crazy Canuck invasion of the Alps, scoring the rare double of Wengen and Kitzbuehel in 1980

a situation unheard of ten years ago – ski-racers from cities, let alone Canada, challenging to be the world's best!

What happened to the Alpine mountain boys who were such a dominant force in Alpine skiing? Simply, they fell victim to a sport that now commands world-wide appeal. The sport now reflects that broad participation. Who, ten years ago, would have thought Canada would possess one of the most powerful men's downhill teams? Or that a Russian, Swede and American would be making virtually a clean sweep of the men's technical events? Certainly not the traditional powers.

It is a very significant trend. The exciting possibility exists for an athlete from any winter nation to be competitive on the world tour if he or she has the desire and drive. That is what will continue to make the sport interesting. Always a new direction, a constant change. The thrill of speed, danger to a degree, and the challenge it all makes to the athlete. Ski-racing is a fascinating sport, and yet one that can be enjoyed by all, whether as a recreational or a competitive skier. The ever-changing challenge is at all levels and the limits are only the ones you put on yourself.

6

GLAMOUR AND GRAFT
Women's Skiing

Divina Galica

Women's racing has occasionally produced exceptional athletes and of all the World Cup winners Annemarie Moser-Proell certainly was in a class of her own. Annemarie, an extrovert at the best of times, won a staggering thirty-six downhills during the nine years she was racing. She amazed everyone by 'retiring' for one season, partly because she fell out with her Federation about whether or not her husband should accompany her to the races. A year later she returned and immediately started to win again. It will be interesting to see whether her sister Cornelia will be able to come anywhere near emulating these achievements. I doubt it although there have been some pretty strong sister combinations competing over the years. Marielle and Christine Goitschel and Brit and Ingrid Lafforgue from France and the Cochran sisters from USA were the duos I had to cope with when I was racing. More recently the Mittermaiers, Evi and Rosi, and Irene and Maria Epple from West Germany. Maria Epple has only just returned to winning form after a devastating injury to her knee which put her out for two years, although sister Irene kept their name to the fore in her absence.

Injury unfortunately is an occupational hazard of the sport and very early on in their careers a lot of girls have learned to grit their teeth and fight back from bad accidents. Of course most people associate the worst accidents with downhill racing but I used to find that a crashing fall in a special slalom could hurt far more, as you collect the poles across your shins, than bowling head over heels down a slope at 60 mph as you might in a downhill. Of course downhill is more frightening as once you set off from the top it is difficult and usually unwise to try and stop before the finish, so although you can slow your speed fractionally by standing upright there is no baling out half-way without a fall.

On the subject of fear I defy even the top downhillers to say they have never felt this emotion, particularly on icy courses when you tend to feel totally out of control. This, combined with pre-race nerves and, having shed all one's warm over-clothes, standing at the start of a downhill, one can feel almost naked, the colourful catsuit being about as much use as a coat of paint. One of the

Divina Galica: not the only skier to switch to motor-racing with experience gained in Alpine passes

downhillers who never seems to show any anxiety before a race is Marie-Therese Nadig, the Swiss who managed on several occasions to defeat the indomitable Moser-Proell and finally last season realised her ten-year-old ambition by winning the elusive World Cup title. Critical followers of the sport will say that she won it in the absence of her two main rivals, Annemarie, who retired after the 1980 Olympics, and Hanni Wenzel, absent for half the season owing to injury. However, I admire the tenacity which kept Marie-Therese near the top of this demanding sport for ten years.

Another 'veteran', Kathy Kreiner, found the strain of training with the younger skiers in the Canadian team so disconcerting that with the blessing of her Federation she employed her own trainer and set up on her own. The first year of this experiment has not produced the kind of results that Kathy might have hoped for and I think the Canadians have found a new star in the attractive Gerry Sorensen, winner of the Haus downhill, and Kathy, who once earned herself a ticker-tape parade in her home town after winning a gold medal in the 1976 Olympics, has unwittingly put herself out to grass.

Training and living with an all-female ski team can be extremely tense at times. Life tends to revolve around the trainer, who is almost always male, and his praise or criticism becomes supremely important. It is difficult for him not to favour the

better skiers, especially the up-and-coming younger ones, and a lot of bitter jealousy can occur. At times the men's and women's teams train together but it is not always possible as men cut different ruts in the courses and after a couple of runs it becomes too difficult for a girl to cope without the possibility of injury. So the harmony of the team weighs heavily on the trainer's shoulders and he needs to be a good psychologist as well as a good skier. I don't think men are quite so affected by their trainers and in particular they seem to be able to cope better with pre-race nerves. Success, of course, is a great confidence-booster and no one proved this more than Hanni Wenzel, who blossomed after her World Cup win. People had difficulty in associating the effervescent character with tinted hair with the rather shy person she had been before. Rosi Mittermaier was another very shy individual, and so superstitious that she refused to change her ski boots until they literally fell apart because they brought her 'good luck'. Rosi, who made a contract with Mark McCormack after she won her World Cup and Olympic medals, certainly cashed in on her success, but then, as someone explained to me, she is everyone's favourite daughter. Her charm has been one of Germany's best exports.

It is difficult to say how far women's success is marketable after retiring from racing. I know that Salomon bindings admitted to having Annemarie under contract for several years after her retirement but were not certain how they were going to use her. A racer is far more important to a company whilst actively pursuing the sport, and a great many of the top girls have substantial contracts with equipment firms, which enables them to earn through their Federation's Ski Pool and protect their amateur status. One of the girls who has made herself more famous since she stopped racing is Susie Chaffee, who competes in freestyle competition in the United States and has perfected an extremely graceful ballet routine. She once drew the world's press to her attention by competing clad in what appeared to be nothing more than her birthday suit. This daring though somewhat cold escapade has made her quite a celebrity and she travels far and wide to demonstrate her skiing ballet, though she now favours exotic costumes much to the disappointment of her fans.

On the whole the most successful women racers tend to be extroverts. Like other sportswomen they share the dedication to gruelling fitness schedules, but unlike a lot of sports they have to add to this a sort of bravado which can be mistaken for fearlessness. They are also toughened by the constant storms and extremes of temperature in the mountains, though I must say I never got used to feeling cold and still wish someone could invent a successful heated ski boot.

However, anyone who has skied will know what an addictive sport it can become and, in spite of the weather and the extremely hard training needed to race at the top, it is a very glamorous life. There are about thirty races during the season, and these are held in classic resorts worldwide such as Val d'Isère, Megève or Aspen where invariably the teams stay in some of the best hotels. They have priority on the lifts and are followed by an army of representatives from the

Speed sisters. *Left:* Annemarie Moser-Proell: successful racers tend to be extroverts.
Right: Cornelia Proell: something to follow

All-time great: Moser-Proell en route to her Lake Placid downhill triumph

Hanni Wenzel. *Left:* Hair fashionably streaked she gives a poised interview at Lake Placid.
Right: The young Hanni

Susie Chaffee: more of a celebrity out of her racing suit than in it

North American success: Tamara McKinney (*left*), at nineteen an American girl to challenge for the top, and Gerry Sorensen, Canadian winner in her first season

major equipment manufacturers to ensure that their preference in skis, boots and bindings are readily available and in perfect condition. They are loaned cars to cart everything around and these are often raced through the icy mountain roads between resorts. Certainly I am not the only skier to have turned to motor-racing with experience gained in the Alpine passes.

Until she retires I think that Hanni Wenzel will continue to dominate the World Cup series despite her setback last year. She too has been at the top of the sport for nearly ten years and that experience counts for a lot in this tough, exciting sport. If I had to choose a young up-and-coming girl to challenge her, I would select 19-year-old Tamara McKinney from the United States, though of course the Austrians, who almost treat skiing as a religion, are bound to replace Annemarie before too long with one of the thirty girls they have standing in the wings.

7

THE WOMEN'S BATTLE

John Samuel

The day Divina Galica effectively exchanged the ski wax room for the motor-racing pits, a cherubic 17-year-old from Flims, in the Swiss Alps, switched out of her soccer jersey into a ski-racer's suit. The day was 8 February 1972, the place Mount Teine in Japan, and it was memorable in the life of Marie-Therese Nadig for her second Olympic gold medal, the giant slalom to add to the downhill. Where Divina was seventh, 'skiing like a madwoman', Marie-Therese was the victor by less than a tenth of a second over Annemarie Moser-Proell. Austria, angered and humiliated by the expulsion of Karl Schranz from those Games, were mortified further by the Swiss unknown's triumph over the hottest favourite of the six Alpine skiing events, indeed blaming Avery Brundage's action for Annemarie's 'failure'.

Over the next eight years the rivalry of Marie-Therese and Annemarie ebbed and flowed. Mostly, for the Swiss girl, it ebbed. Partly making up for her Olympic disappointment, Annemarie won the World Cup overall in 1972 (she had also won it in 1971) and the following three years. And though Annemarie of the iron thighs and steel will temporarily retired for the 1976 Innsbruck Games, the last person to profit was Marie-Therese, confined to bed with a raging temperature on the very eve of the downhill.

The flowering that occurred was not for Flims but for Reit im Winkl, the little Bavarian Alpine village whose eponymous heroine was the girl with the pitter-patter name, Rosi Mittermaier. Rosi won the downhill and special slalom gold medals, lost the giant slalom gold by twelve hundredths of a second to Canada's Kathy Kreiner, and then, with abounding charm and the well-honed words of a champion runner-up, told the world's media men, 'I didn't lose, I was beaten.' Until then Rosi, at twenty-five, had only won six major races, but was placed nineteen times. Partly it was misfortune. In 1973, when well placed for the World Cup, she put herself out of contention with an accident in the Hawaiian surf (ski girls from Reit im Winkl get around). In 1975 a holiday skier bumbled on to the downhill run and into Rosi. That was one more season gone. On the run-in to the

The ups with downs: Marie Therese Nadig (*above*) and Rosi Mittermaier could lose as well as win, but both retired with honours galore

Nadig (*left*): concentrating on soccer. Mittermaier: lucrative marketing contracts – and marriage

Olympics she accomplished the considerable feat of coming last in the Badgastein blizzard. Through a curtain of snow she was heard to yell at one gatekeeper, 'Is everyone going as slow as me?'

Petite, charming and a trim, determined skier, she pursued a longstanding love affair with another West German team member, Christian Neurather, many times a World Cup slalom winner. Everyone on the circuit knew about the affair and said scarcely a word. Rosi's experience of Mark McCormack's hard-driving marketing was lucrative but brief and they all lived happily ever after with Christian and she settling down and marrying, to the delight of a million hausfraus.

Rosi, of course, was as tough as polyurethane ski boots when she had to be, and the press were told very firmly at Innsbruck that, important as Olympic medals were, 'in World Cup you have to be good at all three disciplines in many events all through the season. It is still the better sporting performance.' Then, in case it was too tart for the occasion, she added the truly Olympian sentiment, 'The main thing to remember is not to take sport too seriously. I have learned that because I have been beaten so often.'

Miss Nadig could only go along with that. Her career endlessly obstructed by injury or illness, she was several times on the point of retiring. Having won nothing in 1978–9, suddenly, in Japan again, she jetted away to victory in the Furano giant slalom by 5.2 seconds, an unprecedented margin. She finished fifth overall, but another star had moved into the women's firmament, Hanni Wenzel of Liechtenstein, to obstruct her hopes further. Hanni took the overall title from Annemarie Moser-Proell in 1978 and lost it to the Austrian by only three points in 1979 with the series contested to the very last race. But Marie-Therese was storing herself up for an Olympic season which she opened with an unprecedented set of six downhill victories. Nothing like it had been known since Moser-

Proell's peaks of dominance. With Annemarie twice injuring herself in training and making a sluggish start to the season, the Continental press were full of tales of Marie-Therese's Olympic jinx on the Austrian. But the magic brew boiled dry. Whiteface Mountain, its face stern and unbending like an Indian chief, temperature and wind chill at 25° below and more, was melted not by Marie but by Annemarie, with Hanni slipping between the two for a silver which, with two slalom golds, set her on the same Olympic pedestal as Rosi Mittermaier. 'Mattie' could only rue the scrabrous wind which impeded her more than most.

Hanni, from a country of sixty-one square miles, 24,500 people and 6276 cattle, hair now fashionably streaked, personality and confidence oozing, slipped away from the World Cup field after Lake Placid. Most of Liechtenstein's tales of adventure up to the Wenzels had involved brilliant coups of tax avoidance rather than perilous escapes from fairyland castles. But myth and reality merged joyously in March 1980, as Hanni, with her precise style ('No one is quicker from edge to edge,' Rosi Mittermaier said of her) and square ambition, paired with Andreas to become the first brother and sister winners of the World Cup. Both, together with their 18-year-old sister, Petra, trained with the Swiss team. Once again the Swiss cow bells tolled not for Marie but for Hanni. But Nadig's nine World Cup victories in the season, three more than in the previous eight seasons, were giving her second thoughts about retirement.

Love? Marriage? Soccer? The Swiss press conjectured widely and often wildly on Marie-Therese's future during the brief close season of 1980. Two men were said to be fighting for her – one of the heroes of the men's team on the one hand, an Italian ski area manager on the other. The women's soccer team of Bad Ragaz, near Chur, also called on her passions. But 'Mattie' in the spring was forming her true ambitions. She underwent a shoulder operation and months later the screws were removed. She had fast skis, Blizzard having spent half a million pounds to find a competitive downhill ski again, and an outstanding service man in Dieter Bartsch, a former British team manager and the first Austrian to have such a key role with a prominent Swiss team member. She still enjoyed racing, she was clear of nagging, long-term injury at last, her family were all behind one more effort at winning the World Cup, Moser-Proell had retired. So it was one last crack at the crystal globe. And now it was someone else's turn to be a victim of bad luck – Hanni Wenzel badly injured knee and ankle ligaments in training. Marie-Therese went straight for the throat of her first race, the Criterium of the First Snow downhill at Val d'Isère, and won in a snowstorm.

Quickly she was two downhills, two combineds and a giant slalom to the good, but Altenmarkt, Austria, brought a setback. She tumbled in the downhill training and was sixteenth in the race which was won by the first East European to win a downhill in World Cup, the 21-year-old Czech, Jana Soltysova. Poor Marie-Therese groaned that she could not get any breakfast that morning and so lacked strength, but it was not an endorsement for cereal manufacturers. Falling at 50 mph reduces appetite.

Above: Hanni Wenzel at speed. *Below:* Czechoslovakia's Jana Soltysova, Eastern Europe's first World Cup downhill winner

Above: Doris de Agostini, World Cup downhill runner-up, now favourite for this year's title.
Below: Christine Cooper (USA), fourth overall in 1980–1 and an improving all-round slalomer

Switzerland's Erika Hess: a World Cup slalom record with six successive wins

With her sixth victory of the season, the Crans downhill on 19 January, her lead was 163 to 114 over Perrine Pelen of France. A stream of five special slalom victories by her teammate, Erika Hess, broke a World Cup slalom record, but the Nadig pattern of success in both downhill and giant slalom, with creditable showings in special slalom which she had little enough time to practise, was buttressing her against the inevitable onslaught when Hanni Wenzel returned to the fray. Marie-Therese faltered in Aspen, where the 17-year-old Elisabeth Kirchler won her first downhill for Austria, but the downhill title was already hers with five victories. Furano, the Japanese resort where the sun first rose on her career, was the place where now it would surely set. But not inevitably in triumph. Hanni was now firmly on her track. Victory for Marie-Therese in the giant slalom here would give her the World Cup overall; victory for Hanni would give the Liechstensteiner impetus for the last two races and another triumph on the very tape. The Furano GS course has a 25-second intermediate flat where Nadig's gliding skill tells, but after the first run she was a mere .36 seconds ahead of Wenzel. On the second run she could afford neither to fall nor to miss a gate, but she had to be aggressive or a life's ambition might fail. So what did she do? 'I skied the hell out of my body in the last gates. I took every risk.' And it worked. Nadig was the champ at last. At twenty-seven she could say farewell to ski-racing. Back to a normal life where kicking a soccer ball is one of the major joys.

The Women's Battle 53

8

CHALLENGE FROM THE EAST

John Samuel

Long gone are the days when the Russians saw Alpine skiing as an activity for decadent capitalists. The wind that sprang from the East in January 1980 at Lenggries, West Germany, is now a Force 7 gale which, in 1981–2, a World Championship season, is reaching storm force.

When Peter Popangelov, from Bulgaria, won the slalom in the little German resort, it was hailed as an East European World Cup breakthrough. The great Ingemar Stenmark, three times World Cup overall winner, could only come third. What was missed in all the excitement was the skier who came in second – Alexander Zhirov, 22 at the time, and a Russian. Not, mind you, a Russian from the Caucasus, where there are many high peaks. A Russian from Moscow. A skier trained on a snowy molehill but capable of beating the world's best, as he proved triumphantly in 1981 by winning the last three races of the season.

Zhirov, overall third to Phil Mahre and Ingemar Stenmark, is only one of a clutch of Russians now firmly in the top seed and on the threshold of major accomplishments in both the World Cup series and at Schladming in the World Championships. Valeri Tsyganov won at Aspen in March and finished overall sixth in downhill. Vladimir Andreev was overall seventh in special slalom, one behind Zhirov, who was second only to Stenmark in giant slalom.

The Russians have been around the World Cup circuit since the beginning. They drove the 3000 miles from the Caucasus to the first races at Val d'Isère, in the French Savoie, in an old Russian army truck with an extra motor on the roof in case of breakdown. Their skiers were happy enough in those days to ski the nations' package – a hand-me-down of a couple of places for unqualified skiers. They packed four or five to a room, took what technical assistance Rossignol could offer (though never Western-type deals), and since they were always short of hard currency, tended to take part in all three disciplines for the free digs. Only the lordly Alpine countries could afford the high cost of specialist teams.

But what many overlooked was that only in a strict Alpine ski-racing context could Russia be termed an awakening giant. She entered the Winter Olympic

Bulgarian breakthrough: Peter Popangelov became Eastern Europe's first men's World Cup winner in January 1980

Games for the first time at Cortina in 1956 and at once showed her tradition of cross-country skiing by taking gold. Less obviously, she also took a bronze in women's slalom through Evgenia Soderova. But not only Napoleon and Hitler were capable of overlooking that Russia is a snow country. Because she has no ski resorts readily open to the world, her Alpine reputation languished.

At Russia's back, however, was not only a vast population in snow latitudes, but an entire philosophy embracing the sportsman as a representative of the state. Alpine ski-racing is not simply a recreation, a living or a televisual entertainment. The Russians entered ski-racing ultimately to win, and as such they are likely to become as formidable as an Austrian team supported by the full apparatus of tourist and equipment industry, plus quasi-governmental support.

Stenmark proved that the Alpine countries had no monopoly of ski gold medals and titles. He, too, learned on a molehill without major financial back-up. Leonid Tyagachev, who took over as senior coach of the Russian team in 1975, had first to overcome his team's depression at what seemed to be the overwhelming resources of Austria, Switzerland, Italy and the others, and to point to Stenmark's emergence from a lonely base. The French under Honoré Bonnet introduced summer training in the 1960s. By the seventies all were looking to the Alpine glaciers and the extra snow time. The Russians had plenty of their own – the Mount Elbrus glacier in the Caucasus, the Lago Naki Plateau where snow lies almost freakishly until mid-August. In autumn and winter they could train on the extinct volcanoes of Kamchatka or in the Urals, the Carpathians or the polar regions. Soon the Russians had developed a fitness regimen which exploited the knowledge of other sports disciplines. Soon they were finding first-class racers, like Vladimir Makeev,

Russia's Vladimir Andreev: second place to Stenmark in the Kitzbuehel slalom in his third World Cup season

Sasha Zhirov showed the weight of the Soviet challenge with four victories in the last five races

Valeri Tsyganov, Russia's ace downhiller, surprised the ski world by winning at Aspen

who finished ninth in the 1978 World Championship downhill, and Valeri Tsyganov, who from start number 72 in the 1980 Olympic giant slalom skied into sixth place on the first run. Only a mistake on the third from last gate of the second run cost him a medal. And Tsyganov, strictly, is a downhiller without serious GS training. Makeev has achieved fame in the Soviet Union because he has made the top three in World Cup after being turned down for specialist training because he was 'too old'. The Alpine ski school in the miners' town of Mezhdurechensk in Siberia told him this when he was ten.

Sasha Zhirov learned his skiing ABC a little earlier. He was eight when he started skiing at Tourist, the nearest railroad station to Moscow with a slalom hill nearby. Zhirov was spotted by Victor Talyanov, twenty times a national title-holder, who believed the young boy with the icy-blue eyes had something extra. Zhirov, like Stenmark, has original style and a great ability to 'see' a course. He is a quick, phlegmatic character who assesses his chances coolly. In 1978–9 he analysed the gap between himself and Stenmark and said of the season, 'In principle I am set to win the European Cup.' It was a confident and successful forecast in slalom. No one wanted to win races more than Phil Mahre and Stenmark at the end of last season as they went head to head for the World Cup title. The tall, thin Zhirov responded by winning the final three giant slaloms and the last special slalom. The Russian reputation for workload – about 30% more training than anyone else – is now under challenge as teams seek the Antipodean and glacier snows of summer and winter training and racing. The 1981–2 season is set for a major confrontation between the old powers and the new.

Challenge from the East 57

9

VIEWING SKIING

John Samuel

Millions now watch World Cup racing on television. The commentator has only seconds to identify the racer and get in essential facts. Action often occurs faster than words can tell. But non-skiing armchair viewers can still keep abreast by knowing what to look for.

In the starting gate

Not every telecast shows the start, but where it does the racer's state of mind may be judged. How is he moving around? Is he hyped up? What is his concentration like? Does he look confident? You can see Ken Read's determination by his expression. Ken is quick and nervous on his skis, but full of aggro and challenge. His fellow Canadian, Steve Podborski, is much quieter, both mentally and on his skis. Ingemar Stenmark changes a lot. Sometimes he is nervous and fidgety, at others more relaxed. It depends on the pressure of the course or the time of season. Stenmark likes best to be angry. So did Annemarie Moser-Proell. Phil Mahre is a great competitor, but composed and concentrated in the box. He looks ready to go through a concrete wall. Tune yourself into the racer and you get a better feeling for his run, whether triumph or disaster or something in between. His frame of mind is likely to determine his performance. See if you can read him.

The top of the course

Most skiers adopt the getaway technique perfected by Jean-Claude Killy over fifteen years ago. Under the rules their poles must stay planted in the snow and they position them on the far side of the starting wand. They kick their heels backwards and gain momentum to open the wand and start the electronic timing for the run. Racers develop an exact mental picture of the course. Downhillers know the courses and their trickier sections by long acquaintance. Slalomers, giant and special, can only reconnoitre their shorter, more twisty courses on the day, and then purely by observation. They cannot ski them until the race.

In the start gate each racer has a different mental approach. Some won't try to revisualise the course until the last few seconds. The start must be explosive, but the racer should settle into his rhythm instantly. Konrad Bartelski, on his 'home' course of Kitzbuehel, will focus on the turn coming into the Mausfalle, where the racer must carry a lot of speed for the rest of the course. At Wengen some prefer a blank mind for the relatively long, flat expanse at the beginning where they like to get into their rhythm before the course really dives. Val d'Isère is similar, requiring a concentrated but relaxed approach for the top in readiness for the Collombin jump and the compression. At Garmisch the first four gates are crucial – you may not win the race there, for a range of top contenders are bound to take them well, but you can certainly lose it. All-important is the exit velocity. Steve Podborski was not the fastest there in 1980, but he came out like a cannon shell to win the race.

Concentration at the start: Stenmark (*left*) looks composed; Phil Mahre memorises the course; Klammer (*right*) explodes from the box

Italian style: Bruno Noeckler's busy upper body can mislead. From the hips down he is quiet and efficient

At the top, watch for smoothness and quick anticipation. The racer ought not to be forced into a sudden manoeuvre if he is skiing well and reading the course. You have to allow for different styles. The Italian slalomer, Bruno Noeckler, appears to be moving about a lot, but his legs are doing the work and they are free-moving and absorbing the shocks. From the hips down he is quiet and efficient. A person who looks the fastest isn't always. The quieter skier is probably carrying more momentum into the turns. You look to see if he is well centred over his skis and if he is carving his turns well.

Good turns can vary between downhill, special slalom and giant slalom and depend, too, on the snow and terrain. A pure carved turn leaves a fine, thin line on the snow where the inside edge of the outside ski has cut the surface, as opposed to a skidding, fan-shaped arc where the angled sole of the ski has pushed the snow aside. It is the difference between carving a straight segment of melon with your knife or cutting slightly sideways across the face of the fruit. The first operation is quick and clean, the second slow and slurry. The skier – and this applies as much to the recreational skier as the racer – carves the turn by bringing his weight down on the inside edge at precisely the right moment, forcing the arched ski-section beneath the foot into reverse camber. You go round as if on a rail if the turn is well made.

If the ski fails to bite – and you see this especially in the slalom – and side-slips down the hill even a few inches, precious time and momentum are lost. With

Sizzling Slav: Yugoslavia's Bojan Krizaj has amazing powers of recovery

races sometimes won by one hundredth of a second this kind of mistake is often crucial. On a different course all skiers are likely to make some mistakes, so it is important to gauge how it compares with others and how well the skier has fought back from it. The slalomer, Bojan Krizaj of Yugoslavia, is a marvellously athletic fighter who can only be discounted when he is belly up in the snow. A good snapping carved turn on one ski is a natural springboard on to the other ski and a set of quick zig-zag turns down a steep section of a slalom.

Mid course

In many races, downhills especially, viewers are likely to be picking up the racers at an interval point. Sometimes earlier sections are being videotaped and spliced into live action. Downhill courses will have two interval timing points, one about a third of the way down and the other about two thirds. No two courses are of identical length but interval points are unvarying on each. They are chosen by the organisers according to the nature of the course to indicate the differences between the racers at those points. Continental crowds are sharp as tacks at picking up good interval times – their minds seem to have specially programmed computers. Often their cheers from higher up the course are indicators for race announcers, and even television commentators, of a great performance in the making. There is nothing more stirring in sport than this drum roll echoing down the famous Streif at Kitzbuehel.

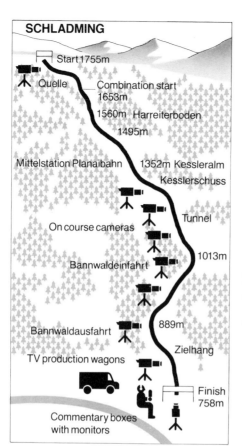

SCHLADMING

- Start 1755m
- Quelle
- Combination start 1653m
- 1560m Harreiterboden
- 1495m
- Mittelstation Planaibahn
- 1352m Kessleralm
- Kesslerschuss
- Tunnel
- On course cameras
- 1013m
- Bannwaldeinfahrt
- 889m
- Bannwaldausfahrt
- Zielhang
- TV production wagons
- Finish 758m
- Commentary boxes with monitors

HOW A RACE IS TELEVISED

Any second now, a downhill racer will come bursting over the top of the mountain, travelling at 80 mph. He'll be difficult to see against the stark white of the snow but the cameraman must pick him up in a split second through the eyepiece of his electronic TV camera, immediately adjust focus so that you at home can see the race clear and sharp. The director shouts through the headphones, 'Swing with him ... zoom in ...' Suddenly the racer has gone ... find the next one ...

In the main TV control wagon (the Scanner) the director is facing a battery of TV screens, one for each camera. He selects his pictures one by one, providing a continuous story of the race which the commentator sees on his monitor in the tiny booth at the bottom of the hill. In the headphones the commentator hears a babble of sound from the director ... from London ... from the recording wagon as a slow motion repeat is suddenly fed in. On goes the race, the time is vital. And back home in Great Britain you sit beside the fire watching one of TV's most exciting sports.

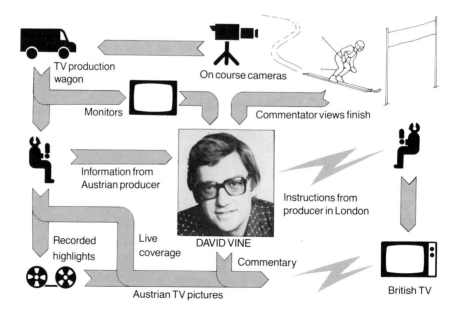

- TV production wagon
- On course cameras
- Monitors
- Commentator views finish
- Information from Austrian producer
- Instructions from producer in London
- Recorded highlights
- Live coverage
- DAVID VINE
- Commentary
- Austrian TV pictures
- British TV

They are privileged in knowing the first interval time, unlike the television viewer who is cued in for the second interval time (there must be a few perks for being on the spot). You see the figures spinning on. Suddenly they stop, and that is the time for the two-thirds mark, and an excellent indicator of how well the racer is doing. The screen will show how he compares with the fastest interval time hitherto. If he's narrowly behind but skiing well he can make up. Then the comparison is with the finish time. Franz Klammer always does better on the lower part of a course. Ken Read at Wengen in 1980 was half a second behind Sepp Walcher but was skiing so well that he won by three hundredths. Someone who skis the bottom third in a way that brings him up from fifteenth place at the second interval to fifth place overall can serve as a guide to good skiing.

The mid and lower sections of the course are usually where the downhill falls come. Here racers are on the limits. Sometimes at 90 mph. Killy had the great art and instinct of staying just inside the limits for the most difficult sections of a course. Others bust them by a fraction – and the results are often spectacular and not a little painful. Of the top fifteen who began 1980–1, a set of famous names were casualties with the season only two thirds over. Not all were race casualties. Uli Spiess, winner of the first downhill at Val d'Isère, was injured in training at Val Gardena. Viewers saw Olympic champion Leonhard Stock disappear into the crowd at Garmisch, coming out of his binding with the race barely started and suffering neck injuries which kept him in a plaster collar for months. Ken Read hurtled out of contention at Garmisch, breaking his nose, sheering one knee ligament and tearing another. He lost his right ski almost immediately, but, as he cartwheeled onwards, the left stayed firmly clamped to his boot. It was the kind of

Faller in the frame: Ken Read cartwheels at Garmisch as televiewers world wide hold their breath

fall that has the binding manufacturers worrying and wondering. Every non-skiing viewer could see the problem. Solving it was another matter.

Peter Mueller, Swiss World Cup downhill champion of 1980 and strongly contending for 1981, was caught by the cameras with a spectacular fall on the final jump of his home course at Wengen. Mueller ended up in the straw bales guarding the finish after landing too far back on his skis and zooming off line. He dislocated a shoulder but made his comeback before the end of the season.

Falls often come when a downhiller presses that fraction too far in the wrong place at the wrong moment, which is why huge crowds congregate at the critical points. Often, downhill falls are the consequence of mistakes made a few moments earlier. By getting off line and over-reacting, being caught out by visibility or perhaps a straight technical error – weight fractionally displaced, too far back or too far forward – in any event, getting off balance. The fight to correct or salvage a run is one of the great spectacles of TV sport. You have to try and pick out the initial error to understand the reasons for a fall, or, much more frequently, the recovery. The question for a top racer is whether the recovery has cost him too much time.

The slalomer is quite capable of blowing the first gate if he lets his concentration wander. Usually, though, a crucial error is followed by another and another as he tries to bring his skis under control. Often he succeeds; but the margins of slalom success and failure are slighter than those of downhill. Occasionally a master slalomer achieves a sublime beauty with a run, as if mind and body have taken wing in unison. Gustavo Thoeni's second slalom run at the 1974 World Championships was such a one. Ingemar Stenmark's second at St Anton on 1 February 1981 was another. It is worth watching a hundred hoppity performances for one such as this.

_The finish

Observe the racer's expression as he skids to a stop. Even before he has seen his time he can often tell the quality of his run. He usually knows better than anyone else how well he has skied. Does he look disappointed? Is he especially tired? But the racer can be wrong. If it is difficult for one top skier it probably will be for the others too. Racers don't set themselves times to beat, even in the second run of a slalom. They just set out to ski as fast as they can: the clock will look after itself. Peter Mueller was clearly delighted with his Kitzbuehel downhill run just before his crash at Wengen. Along came Ken Read with one of the races of his life to win by two seconds. Then it was Kenny's turn to beam and hold his skis aloft. Top skiers know all the promotional ropes. If they're in with a chance their skis are off in the twinkling of an eye and ready for the hand-held TV cameras in the finish area. They know what they owe to their ski manufacturers, and what is expected of them. FIS have tried to ban TV microphones in the finish areas for 1981–2, hoping racers will be given a chance to get their breath before giving interviews.

On the limits at Garmisch: downhillers press to the ultimate on the mid and lower sections.
Under the finish banner the racer knows better than anyone what kind of run

The pressures of good public relations, in which racers are important agents, may defeat them.

Weather

Each year different courses, especially downhill, pose varying challenges because of snow conditions and vision. The first panoramic TV shots will give the clues to the problems: sunshine, cloud, snow, rain, wind, fog, good light, bad light, varying light all come into it. Wengen in sunshine is a marvellous picture. The Lauberhorn downhill starts above the treeline against the background of the Eiger and the Jungfrau and a racer plunging into the forested section of the course is like an express train hitting a tunnel. Trees, though, can be a help when flat light camouflages the bumps and hollows of the snow and the racers have only this and the 'feel' of their boot soles and their skis between them and disaster. On these occasions viewers may see fir sprigs used as visual aids for skiers and cameramen. Sepp Ferstl, West Germany's fourth-placed downhiller at the World Championships in 1978, was a notably bad skier in poor light. Ken Read is notably good.

Snow

Harder to judge, for the armchair viewer, is the snow on which the athletes perform. Scientifically snow is elusive. It is formed high up in the atmosphere when air containing water vapour rises and cools and condenses on to tiny particles of dust or salt. Below freezing point the iced particles grow as more water vapour attaches. The particles get heavier and heavier until they finally tumble down in the form of snow crystals. They may be stars, rods, spikes, needles, plates or an infinite variety of other shapes.

Crystals forming around salt particles, as opposed to dust, will have different characteristics. Vancouver on the coast of British Columbia, Hokkaido on the most northerly island of Japan and Cairngorm in Scotland, close to the Atlantic on one side and the North Sea on the other, will all have a different type of snow to Aspen in Colorado – a thousand miles from the sea in any direction. Hail of the sort which occasionally strikes like anti-aircraft flak on Cairngorm has invariably passed through thick fog or cloud, the cold water freezing on to the crystal and creating a kind of pellet. Ordinary anoraks are hopelessly inadequate against it.

Change in snow goes on and on. As the crystal or flake reaches the ground there is a process called snow metamorphosis. Within a day or two, two feet of snow may be down to a foot. New snow contains about 90% of trapped air. This seeps away and the snow crystal itself changes its form. Almost everyone is delighted by the squeak when trampling new snow. It is literally the sound of crystals being crunched. Once the snow has started to metamorphose the sound does not occur. Surface snow conditions will vary according to time of season, day, location on

Snow-gun salvo: machine snow techniques from the US East are now employed at Aspen and Schladming

the mountain, depth, age and variety of layering. Every few yards will have a different character to which the skier, first with his eye, otherwise by the feel of snow under his skis, must react. No skier will be a champion, whatever his other qualities, without this 'feel'. As Jean-Claude Killy once remarked, 'To be a great skier you must have intelligence of the feet'.

As racers, organisers, sponsors and TV programme controllers grow more demanding, coursemakers grow more sophisticated. Snow is easier to master than the weather itself. If you don't like the snow you change it, or make it yourself. Lake Placid ran an Olympic Games on man-made snow. Marc Hodler, President of FIS, said afterwards it marked a new epoch. 'It's easier to plan Alpine events on man-made than real snow.' North America, especially the Eastern resorts, pioneered machine snow. Europe has just begun to follow. Schladming, near Salzburg, Austria, scene of this season's World Championships, has installed snow guns at the bottom of the men's downhill run to avoid the disastrous wipe-outs of the last two World Cup events staged there. Snowmaking has become a fine art. In essence man-made snow is fine crystals created by atomised water being fired into the air by a 'gun' in sub-zero temperatures. Depending on temperature, humidity, type of snowmaking system and sort of snow required, machine snow can be dry or wet. Killington in Vermont, with snowmaking on forty-three of its

seventy-five trails, including the 62-degree Outer Limit, hosts the US ski team's training as early as November and rightly claims a share in Phil Mahre's glory.

Since less air goes into the making of each flake, one inch of man-made snow equals six inches or more of natural snow. For the 1964 Winter Olympic Games, entire regiments of the Austrian army were employed to shift natural snow to Innsbruck's almost snowless courses. Since then the art of course-making has developed phenomenally, even where machine snow is not available. Chemicals are now used to harden slalom courses and prevent serious rutting to a very late stage of a race. It explains the excellent slalom competitions of 1980–1 where, on a good day, racers with start numbers in the twenties and thirties could expect to challenge the top fifteen.

The two- to three-mile downhills cannot possibly be prepared to the same extent. A lot of snow will fill hollows in the underlying base. Bumps and pitches will be less accentuated. Temperature also comes into it. Cold new snow, providing there is only a foot or so, will provide excellent conditions. Three feet or more will have the organisers ordering squadrons of snow tractors into action, maybe working all night to flail it down ready for the race. Too much snow, these days, is more of a problem than too little. More often in recent seasons the snow has been relatively thin. Viewers should watch for the bumps and hollows and how a racer is mastering them. Is he 'swallowing' them? Is he being thrown?

Temperature and humidity will be measured by the racer's ski technicians at critical points from top to bottom of a major course. Snow conditions will vary enormously over a vertical course of perhaps two miles with a vertical drop of over half a mile. Some sections are in shadow, others in sunlight. The snow will vary with each, and expert waxing is essential to cope with it. Sometimes you see someone skiing as if he had left the handbrake on. This may be a wax disaster. It still happens, although less often with almost every aspect, including the racer's physical characteristics, computerised by the ski company racing experts. Even so, human error intervenes. In 1979 a famous ski company had a virtual wipe-out among their top Austrians and Canadians. Someone put the wrong labels on the wax boxes.

Outer limits: Killington's 62-degree slope, the steepest in the East, hosts Phil Mahre and the US team in training

10

EQUIPMENT

John Samuel

Helmets. Since the 1950s, simple leather helmets, like those of First World War pilots, have become sophisticated items of equipment made of lightweight but strong man-made fibres with foam linings. They are cut high at the back so that the racer can keep his tuck position while lifting his head just enough to see where he is going. Some racers use detachable faceguards. Others find them distracting or liable to make goggles mist.

Goggles. An essential item of any skier's equipment. Recreational or slalom skiers may only use them when it is snowing; downhillers at speeds up to 85 mph must use them constantly. Frames are shaped for use with helmets. Detachable lenses are treated with chemicals to prevent misting up; they come in three main colours: blue-grey for sun, green for medium bright, yellow for fog or snow. Rain will cause the postponement of a downhill if it obscures the racer's goggles.

Suits. A downhiller wears only his underpants beneath his skin-tight suit. It has gone through many evolutions from the dungarees of the early postwar years. In the middle 1970s the Italians introduced rubberised, sheathlike suits which brought them spectacular results and even more spectacular injuries with racers catapulting off courses dangerously when they fell. These were banned by FIS, but so competitive and commercialised was the sport becoming that manufacturers simply rubber-coated the suits inside, and it required a racer rebellion to outlaw them. Racers found themselves sweating so profusely that they were constantly in danger of picking up colds and chills. FIS introduced a rule that suits 'breathed' properly with a minimum fifty litres of air able to pass through one square metre of material per minute. Testing also had to be introduced, and in one famous incident Canada's Ken Read was deprived of first place in a World Cup downhill at Morzine in 1979 because his new suit did not meet the tests. Synthetic fabrics are now used with built-in non-slip properties.

Giant slalom suits are now similar to downhill, with extra padding to cushion knee, thigh and shoulder if they strike the slalom poles. Special slalomers will also use padded jerseys and trousers to prevent bruising.

Bibs. These are now elasticated to cut down wind resistance. All racers must wear bibs giving start numbers to identify them.

Gloves. Some holiday skiers prefer mittens to keep their hands warm. Racers will use padded gloves for more exact hand feel.

Poles. Made of lightweight metal, poles may be less used by a racer than a recreational skier as turning aids, but they remain important balancing items. The downhill pole has a kink half-way down to accord better with his body position when he is in the tuck. Length will be a matter of preference. Downhillers have plastic orbs to prevent the point of the pole catching too deeply in the snow. These assist the aerodynamic qualities built into all their equipment. Slalom poles have baskets to stop them penetrating too deeply in the snow when they are planted to assist turning.

Bindings. A critical item with an extremely delicate, specialised purpose. The binding holds boot to ski, usually by sprung heel- and toe-clips, with sufficient firmness to withstand the shock and jar of bumps and turns between 60 and 85 mph, but with release properties in a fall. In 1980–1 there was no instance of a top racer breaking a leg, but binding makers were seriously concerned by the number of ligament injuries. Racer bindings will have stronger springs than a holiday skier's, which makes them harder to release, and they will be set much tighter. Even so, they should snap open in a serious fall. Bindings will have a variety of settings according to the measure of backwards, forwards, sideways and upwards pressures exerted. The better the skier the tighter the setting. Binding manufacturers employ service teams at every race to check individual settings with scrupulous care.

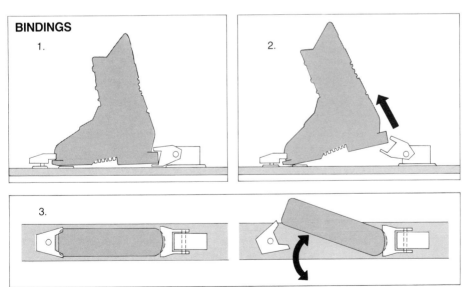

BINDINGS

1. Step-in heel unit before release. 2. Step-in heel unit after release during a forward fall. 3. The action of the toe binding before and after release during a sideways twisting fall.

Boots. Racers treat a boot as part of their person. It is as important as that. Skis and aerodynamic design of equipment and clothes have made ski-racing faster. Boots provide the control that was impossible even ten years ago. Postwar, boots were little different in basic design to a mountain-walking boot. Synthetics, in particular polyurethane, and design techniques have revolutionised the boot shell and its effects, while linings of foam or putty-like substance in its own inner boot have made the shell wearable. Now, leg forces are transmitted with the minimum of energy loss to skis and their edges.

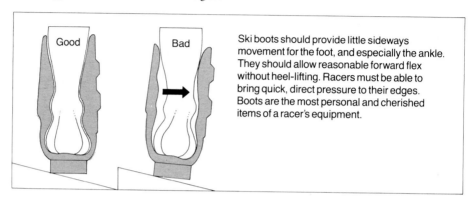

Good

Bad

Ski boots should provide little sideways movement for the foot, and especially the ankle. They should allow reasonable forward flex without heel-lifting. Racers must be able to bring quick, direct pressure to their edges. Boots are the most personal and cherished items of a racer's equipment.

In choosing his boot the racer has to define his needs. His boots will be custom-made and the product of hours of testing. Where the first plastic boots were calf high, today they are rather lower with varying rigidity. The ankle must move backwards and forwards but as little as possible sideways. Downhillers will seek a softer forward flex for their crouched tuck position. But it must be firm enough for gliding or turning on ice. Some racers are bow-legged, others knock-kneed. Ski soles will be wedged accordingly to ensure skis are flat on the snow.

Skis. A ski is a precise tool to support man in his fastest unpropelled activity over land. Its graceful shape precisely determines its function. People fall in love with skis, racers possibly above all. Skis are tailored for particular purposes. In plan view a ski is wide at the front, narrower in the middle and wider again at the tail. In side view it is arched beneath the binding where the skier will bring most of his weight to bear. Standing normally, the skier will force the arch, or camber as it is known in this context, downwards. The effect is for the ski to track in a straight line. With more force still, the ski will bow into the snow in a reverse camber. The sidecut of the inside of the left ski will help a turn to the right, and vice versa. But the ski helps the turn in other ways. Though the weight may in general remain central to the skis, when the knees are pushed forward there will be more pressure on the front of the skis. The shovel of the tip thus will brake, and with any sideways pressure the tail, which is not suffering the check, will fan out. A good skier will be using a set of forces such as these in combination and with precise timing.

The Alpine ski-maker uses a complex sandwich of metal, wood and synthetics

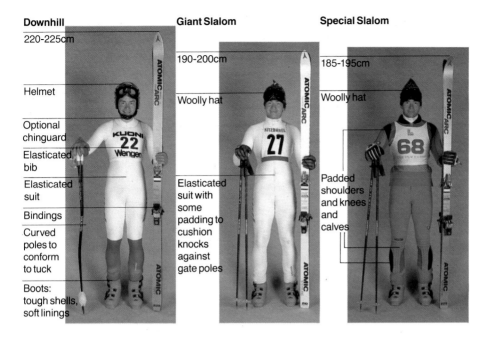

Downhill	Giant Slalom	Special Slalom
220-225cm	190-200cm	185-195cm
Helmet	Woolly hat	Woolly hat
Optional chinguard		
Elasticated bib		
Elasticated suit	Elasticated suit with some padding to cushion knocks against gate poles	Padded shoulders and knees and calves
Bindings		
Curved poles to conform to tuck		
Boots: tough shells, soft linings		

to achieve the best object for the purpose. The downhill ski must track straight and fast for most of its journey. It will be 220 to 225 centimetres long (seven feet or more), and 200 to 210 for women, with less sidecut for longer turns and stiffish middle tail so that it runs without excessive vibration on hard snow and changing terrain. One make of downhill skis has a hole the size of a tennis ball in the tip. The hole is to reduce the weight mass of the extremely flat tip, which is designed to improve flex, and thus handling. Being so vulnerable to breakage, this design is used only by racers.

Giant slalom skis are 205 to 210 centimetres long (190 to 200 for women), with more pronounced sidecut and camber to achieve more turn with less effort. Special slalom skis, 200 to 207 centimetres (185 to 195), are quicker-reacting still, with more sidecut and camber.

Makers will go to the lengths of computerising skis and skiers to get the right ski for the right man or woman. A heavier skier will require different characteristics to a light one. One ski maker has a course wired up to skis which flash different lights according to the amount a skier uses his edges, the slim metal borders to his ski base. Sharp metal edges assist turning in compacted snow or ice, but are a drag compared with the rest of the waxed base. In soft snow skiers may file down their edges. Downhill racers, or their advisers, will select from six different polyethylene bases the one which best suits snow conditions. Their ski manufacturer will have had a team out on the mountainside measuring snow characteristics and temperatures. A top racer will have fourteen pairs of skis travelling around with him, including six main pairs, six duplicates for training runs, and two general-

purpose pairs, including one for free skiing. At the last, before a big race, a top skier will have a pair presented to him, all the decisions made by his ski company's racing manager and his country's chief downhill coach. His job is to win.

Wax is used on ski bases to make them run faster and turn better. The movement of skis on snow produces friction and warmth, which makes the snow melt. A snow crystal has six points and new snow will be sharp, roughening the wax coating: a hard wax is therefore necessary. As snow ages it loses shape, becoming rounded and granulated. The change happens fast if the temperature rises and the snow starts its change into water. Some parts of a course in shade or between trees will change less quickly than exposed slopes. Steep sections will be less hard on wax than flat. Over two miles there are bound to be differences. So race waxers must take account of a variety of conditions when choosing, which accounts for use of a computer in the choice of the wax layers. The foundation wax must be able to cover the widest range of temperatures and snow conditions likely to be found on the course. With increasing sophistication, the 'wax race', won not by the best skier but the one with the best wax, has become almost a thing of the past.

11

HOW RACES ARE RUN

John Samuel

Downhill

Downhill is a race of not less than two minutes for men and one minute 40 seconds for women, which must test a racer's technique, agility, concentration, endurance, fitness and courage. It is decided on best time, the clock measuring hundredths of a second until the lower half of either leg cuts a photo-electric beam at the finish. FIS decree that it must be possible to slide the course without use of ski poles. The terrain must be cleared of stones, tree-stumps and all similar obstacles which might create danger when snow is thin. Control gates must be used to prevent speeds becoming dangerous, with the Technical Delegate from FIS the ultimate authority.

In common with special slalom and giant slalom each race is controlled by a jury consisting of the Technical Delegate, who serves as chairman, a referee, an assistant referee appointed by team captains, start referee, finish referee and the chief of race. The jury checks courses, safety measures and crowd control, reviews gate setting, conducts the draw for start places on the eve of a race, and has power to postpone, cancel or shorten a race depending on conditions.

Courses, usually between two and three miles for men and one and a half to two for women, must be a minimum of 20 metres (65 ft) wide and 30 metres (98 ft) at more dangerous points. Pairs of flags, red for men's courses and alternate red and blue for women's, act as 'gates' which must be set to limit speeds and guide competitors past tricky and dangerous points. Direction flags are red on the left-hand side of a course and green on the right. If visibility is poor, pine sprigs may be scattered on the course as visual bearings. The vertical drop should be 800–1000 metres (2624–3280 ft) for men and 500–700 metres (1542–2296 ft) for women. The slope should average 30 to 35 degrees although some gradients will be 50 degrees or more. A shorter downhill, with unspecified vertical drop, is now incorporated in World Championship programmes to couple with a special slalom race for a 'combined' event.

Cecil Hopkinson was the winner of the first recognised downhill race, the Roberts of Kandahar, run by the British Public Schools Alpine Sports Club at Crans-Montana, Switzerland, in 1911. He climbed for seven hours, then, the following morning, descended the three miles of glacier and 4000 feet of untracked mountainside to beat his nine rivals. He stopped on the way for a drink and to pass the time of day with friends, but completed the course in one hour one minute to justify the backers in his Montana hotel who had made him 4–1 favourite.

Amid increasing sophistication, downhill became a test of speed and daring, and slalom (from the Norwegian, meaning a track down a smooth hill) of turning and technique. Downhill and slalom in combination became an Olympic event at Garmisch-Partenkirchen in 1936. Austrian and Swiss skiers were banned because of professionalism. In their absence the world jumping champion, Birger Ruud, spending some business time in the Alps, won the downhill in 4:47.4; his average speed was 29.74 mph. On 14 February 1980 an Austrian reserve, Leonhard Stock, won the Olympic downhill at Lake Placid in 1:45.50 over a course of 3009 metres, or just over two miles. It was about half a mile shorter, but the average speed was 64.17 mph.

The difference can be summed up in better course preparation, harder surfaces, better skis and wax, more aerodynamically sophisticated suits, sticks and helmets, improved technique, better fitness, greater mental awareness, a service back-up ranging from doctors to videotapers, rewards of cash from an intensive ski industry, and worldwide prestige which the media and, above all, television confer. The 'take' for the victor of a modern World Cup downhill will not be less than $50,000 in direct and indirect terms. Comparisons of course times in themselves are misleading. It depends on snow and weather conditions from year to year; from minute to minute even. If one aspect remains constant, it is the courage of the men who practise downhill. Hazards are nothing new. Most of the ten rivals for the Roberts of Kandahar Cup in 1911 fell repeatedly on the 1500 feet of steep, hard, windswept snow below the Col de Thiery.

Why, then, do people do it? There is the simple pleasure of competition which skiers get at the most elementary level in handicap races in the US, and now in Britain. Virtually any skier can test his skill on a relatively easy course against the time of a local star who has earned a handicap by skiing at the beginning of each season against the very best. Racing builds skills. It teaches you to turn where the course-setter demands, and not when it is most convenient. It teaches you to make more efficient turns in all kinds of snow surfaces. It provides an adrenalined circumstance where you can hope to achieve your best, so that you can break through real and imagined barriers for a sense of self-fulfilment. It gives fitness routines a frame and an object. Finally it can be a challenge to self – literally man against the mountain, rather than man against man. It explains the mutual respect among racers which, in spite of the hero worship and rewards that attach to the success of the top few, soars far above crude nationalism and envy.

Olympic champion: Austria's Leonhard Stock wins the Lake Placid downhill at an average speed of 64.17 mph

A downhiller is about 180 lbs of highly trained body mass compressed into a pair of paper-light underpants and $\frac{1}{16}$th of an inch of skin-tight aerodynamic nylon suit. On his head is the one item of protection – a helmet of reinforced plastic with a foam-rubber lining. Some will favour a mouth guard. The pursuit of hundredths of a second means super-lightweight gloves, sticks curved for minimum wind resistance, boots fared with the same object and clipped, most of them, at the back out of the wind line, goggles streamlined, even the ventilation holes taped over, and skis honed and tuned from a set of a dozen for this precise two–minute job.

Racers will cherish their skis better than their best girl friend. Downhill skis are much longer than those used for slalom and giant slalom (see p.94). The skis are the essential contact with the snow of this overall 220 lb projectile seeking all the forces of gravity in pursuit of its mission to be fastest down a mountainside. Steve Podborski, breaking the Garmisch record on 10 January 1981, hit 90 mph. That is 35 mph above the legal maximum of US autoroutes, 20 mph above British, and no enveloping upholstery and metal, only two narrow, bumping, chattering skis which you must control or risk disaster. Skiing gives man his fastest form of locomotion without mechanical aid. Among skiers, the downhiller is supreme.

How Races are Run 77

The 24th Arlberg–Kandahar on the Kreuzeck above Garmisch in January 1959 was formative. The course at 3.4 kilometres was not particularly long or difficult. However, the light turned flat, a circumstance in which skiers seek their bearings in a grey half-world without depth or proper reference. Trees float by as if on a frieze. They are moving; you are still. Then a bump and your knees are up to your jaw, and you can only struggle to get forward and keep your balance. Three forerunners were to test the course. Two never made the bottom. The third did so, but fell four times.

In his book, *Ski Racing*, Curtis Casewit chronicled the rest. Anderl Molterer, one of the great Austrians, came first. 'He was white like paper and when he pulled off his crash helmet his blond hair remained glued green to his forehead. He summed up this Kandahar with one word, "Madness!"' Willy Forrer of Switzerland arrived shaking, just murmuring 'Oh God, oh God!' Then the winner, Karl Schranz, a baby of twenty-one for those days, pale, but acknowledging, 'I'm alive'. As the race went on the casualties ticked up like a Flying Fortress raid on Schweinfurt. Eighty-nine starters, thirty-nine fallers. Casewit reported, 'There were altogether six broken limbs, two broken ribs and one ripped-off nose – cleanly sheared to the upper lip, bone and all.' Racer No. 44, John Semmelink of Canada, 20 years old, made it half-way down in perfect form, legs like steel. 'He was still sliding down through the chutes at high speed, jumped down the "Ice Wall", sped hotly through the narrow "Holle" [Hell], and then entered the "Himmelreich" [Heaven]. Witnesses later reported that he took a turn too fast. One of his bindings opened: he fell high through the sky and crashed into a 300-foot gully. It was icy and studded with rocks. His helmet broke like an eggshell.' Semmelink died three hours later.

Toni Mark, a promising young Austrian, died when he catapulted into rocks in the same year. It was thought to be a hazard of the game. Even in 1964, when the Australian, Ross Milne, somersaulted into trees during practice for the Innsbruck Winter Games, there were some who tried to explain away the lack of adequate safety netting by suggesting that countries like Australia should not be competing in downhill. Subsequently Milne's brother, Malcolm, was to place in the first three of a World Cup race and silence the critics. The world ski-racing map had changed out of all recognition by the 1980s.

Of up to 100 people shooting one by one from the downhill starting-gate, at intervals of up to two minutes, the first fifteen in normal conditions will be the crème de la crème – the top fifteen in FIS rankings and departing in order of a draw made the night before. The remainder start according to FIS rankings issued three times a year and based on a racer's best two performances in any given period. The only variation to this comes in World Cup races, where a quota of all-round skiers is permitted to race after the first fifteen to get the advantage of good snow for combined points. Every racer has a minimum of three training runs, including one non-stop timed trial, before a World Cup race. Most use practice to test various sections of the course, with team helpers videotaping key

The back-up teams: behind every racer a set of trainers, service men, video recorders, medics and other helpers

sections for the racers and their coaches to pore over in the privacy of their hotels. With a maximum of four competitors per nation allowed in Olympic Games and World Championship races and ten (plus an extra six for the host nation) in World Cup, the major Alpine nations, with A, B and C cadres of furiously competing racers, sometimes opt for selection according to practice performance. Austria, under Karl Kahr in particular, adopt this procedure, but the elimination of famous names introduces heavy controversy.

In extraordinary conditions, for example with heavy snow falling, a group of at least six competitors from the back of the field may be required to run before No. 1. They are chosen by draw from the last twenty per cent, and are expected to provide a fairer track for the top seeds together with the forerunners who precede them. There are not less than three forerunners, or vorläufers as they are more usually known in Europe, and they are expected to follow a good racing line and provide information as necessary to the jury.

The preparations for 100 racers trying to crack two minutes on a downhill course are costly and formidable. Top racers are full-timers. Their season barely ends in March or April before they are back into summer training. (Those, including the Canadians, who race in the Southern Hemisphere season in Australia and New Zealand have shown impressive sharpness for the European World Cup season in December. South America, and Portillo in Chile in particular, also provides a training base.) In the ten World Cup and one World Championship downhills of the 1981–2 season a racer will not be on course much

more than twenty-two minutes. That, superficially, is his year's work. Behind it, though, will be thousands of hours of explosive and endurance training, ski and wax testing and glacier and other high-mountain training.

Behind a British racer on a two-minute downhill are a back-up team of at least a dozen, the secretariat included, and Britain is only a third division Alpine power. The chief reason for this is not a smaller administration and back-up or that Britain has few ski centres compared with the Alpine countries. Britain has many ski enthusiasts – its pioneers can be said to have invented the game – but it has skiers first and athletes second. The Alpine countries have athletes who are skiers. They have succeeded at every level, from junior onwards, because they are good athletes, with a proven physiology and psychology for the job. Most top skiers, slalomers as well as downhillers, strip like well-made boxers. This applies to Czechs, Yugoslavs and Spaniards as well as Austrians, Swiss, Germans and Italians. The US has mountains and more than fifteen million regular skiers, but, until the Mahre twins, America has struggled to match the Alpine countries. Canada has broken through only in the last five years, and then, as far as the men are concerned, only in downhill. Their women, in a less competitive field, have a rather longer record of success, including Nancy Greene, World Cup overall winner in 1967 and 1968, the first two seasons.

A downhill skier's efforts to defy gravity last about 120 seconds, but each second is split into a hundred parts as the official timing provides. If there are 12,000 parts to a course of 12,000 feet, such as the famous Streif at Kitzbuehel, then one small mistake – the mistaken press of a ski edge, a little too hard, a little too soft, a little too early, a little too late – may make the difference between a first and second place. Not much more and you are among the also rans of the thirties and forties.

It has taken a mighty effort for Canada to catch up. The team spends about £15,000 for every racer in Europe. The Norwegians estimate it costs £5000 a man simply to train. A top coach will cost £20,000 a year. Always they are chasing Alpine countries, Austria, Italy and Switzerland especially, whose economies depend to varying degrees on tourism. Austria produces more skis annually than the rest of Europe put together; also one and a half million ski and mountain boots and a million sets of ski bindings. Little wonder that she finds the financial resources to ensure that by fourteen – the FIS legal minimum – no good youngster has escaped the net. Schools of physical culture at Schladming and Stams combine ski-racing with other education (Harti Weirather went to Stams) and are wedded to the system. The methodology grows ever more sophisticated. Early puberty at one time rewarded the precocious. Now the Austrians seek also to catch the late developers in an all-embracing programme.

All racers make mistakes. The winner is the racer making the fewest and least serious errors. A near-perfect run with one serious mistake can drop a skier into the also-rans. It happened to Steve Podborski at St Anton in January 1981 when he needed one more victory to secure the World Cup downhill title. He slid too

Each course will set its special traps: Franz Klammer lives dangerously in the St Anton
Arlberg-Kandahar

wide on one of the early turns, and third place might just as well have been 103rd.
To capture and harness all the forces of gravity against wind and weather, bumps
and hollows, pitches and flats, a downhiller has one goal – to stay in the tuck, or
egg, position for as much of the course as is possible. The tuck is what his hours of
exertion are primarily about.

Each course will set its special traps. Each has its own personality, its charm,
oddities, indeed beauties. There is no reference to the Streif at Kitzbuehel among
top racers – especially the aces who have learned to respect it most – without a
sense of awe. You observe its nave and flying buttresses as you might St
Stephen's in Vienna, Bach's Toccata and Fugue echoing in your head. It has the
Mausfalle (Mouse Trap) at the start where the racer takes off as if into a void. To
win there, as Ken Read did in 1979, was the summation of a career. To achieve it,
though, he had to accomplish the incredible athletic feat of staying crouched,
calves virtually at right angles to his skis, thighs at another right angle to the
calves, for most of the two and a quarter miles with its vertical drop of 2830 feet,
or about one in four.

Downhillers develop thighs as big as many men's waists. Less obvious are the
back muscles. As Peter Mueller hits the compression at Val d'Isère, and every
force of gravity, the 'Gs', tries to push his knees up into his belly, the video film

will show the flexing of his enormous back muscles. The landings at the Collombin jump at Val d'Isère, or the Kamelsprunge (Camel Jumps) at Val Gardena are like jumping from a second-floor office window. And the downhillers do the equivalent every day, six times a day. Most of the pressure is absorbed through the back; all the co-ordination necessary for the entire extraordinary activity passes through it. Many recreational skiers have tried wall-sits to prepare themselves for a new season. One minute back to the wall, thighs out straight, is enough for most. The downhiller in the tuck suffers the strain of two minutes of thighs plus back in an opposed but similar stress situation. Travelling at 60 to 90 mph against all the buffets of wind, bump and hollow, it is like riding the 'egg' position with a 220-lb man riding piggy-back on your shoulders.

Downhill skis are soft at the tip to absorb bumps, fairly stiff in the middle and very stiff at the tail. You have to keep your skis on the snow as much as possible. Time in the air is time forfeited, although a certain amount is inevitable. The downhiller does not look a stylist. He keeps a widish track, about a shoulder wide, and anticipates a bump by retracting his legs and keeping his arms well down. He appears to be leaning back slightly, but this is an illusion. He pushes his feet down fast after the bump. Energy is stored in the stiff ski-tails and he wants maximum acceleration as he shoots forward on contact with the ground. Hand and arm positioning are critical. Pushing a hand out of the window of a car travelling at 80 mph shows the force of the wind at this speed. The smallest untoward movement at this speed has damaging effects. If a racer crouched at 85 mph suddenly stood up he would be flipped right over. No one would be so mad, but an arm and stick thrown out of body line can seriously check the chances of winning, or simply a good finishing time.

If the downhiller's chief aim with his body posture is to stay in the tuck, his main object with his feet is to ride a flat ski. On a side hill he will by instinct and training roll his ankles over to keep the ski flat. He will try to swallow a bump. The technique of pre-jumping, the effort to jump fractionally before a bump to avoid being thrown into the air to a degree that seriously slows him, has been refined. Most racers now try to retract their legs with a jack-knifing effect. This enables them to stay low. As quickly as possible over the bump he thrusts his legs downwards and is back into a full tuck and flat ski. Birds landing on water have something of the same technique. His eyes focus on key points – a turn, a bump, a tree – perhaps 200 feet away. He's ready, like a driver at an intersection, for the check or directional change, then a fix on the next sign or mark. His body is being programmed by his vision – swiftly and exactly.

Britain's Konrad Bartelski, unhappy with his mind and body processes for just this object, played hours of golf to improve his concentration. Steve Podborski trains with his brother, a top cyclist, to improve his process. Soccer is a game played almost universally by top skiers because it improves eye and muscle co-ordination. The Austrians and Yugoslavs are perhaps the most notable. Klammer and Werner Grissman are good competition drivers. Psychologically they must

DOWNHILL TECHNIQUES

Downhill turns
The two main types are: 'Austrian' turn with inside ski notably lifted and outside ski heavily weighted (1). The Orthodox high speed turn (2). The outside ski does most of the work, the tail of the ski weighted with the heel as with the Austrian turn. The inside ski is almost flat on the snow.

The tuck position
Basic crouched position, aerodynamically streamlined, which racers seek to achieve throughout the race, riding the flattest possible ski.

1.

2.

Swallowing a bump
Legs are retracted, if necessary with a jump anticipating the bump (often described as a pre-jump). The legs are quickly extended again to regain snow contact. Time in the air is time lost.

be on top of themselves. Mind, in the end, will control matter. Podborski had an outstanding season in spite of a serious knee injury. Peter Patterson, the US downhiller, had a bone splinter rattling around his knee like ice in a cocktail shaker before an operation in February put things right. After badly hurting knee ligaments, Hanni Wenzel started World Cup only in January but still finished third. Phil Mahre, outstandingly, came back from a complex leg fracture to win the World Cup, finishing as high as ninth in one downhill.

The strength of mind and technical skills of a slalomer must never be under-rated. Phil Mahre did the damage to his ankle in 1979 in slalom. But downhill is the prime test of courage and endurance and its turns demand a technique of their own. Thrown by a bump, the downhiller should still try and hang on to his crouch. It is the same at a turn. His outside ski is thrust powerfully into the snow by his knee. Centrifugal force bananas the inside edge of that ski and round he goes on the waisted side-cut of the ski edge. The inside ski, meantime, stays more or less flat on the snow. If a turn is made in a more upright position – and Austrian downhillers in particular tend to be less crouched – the hips must angulate more. The outside ski and leg do most of the work, with the tail of the ski a little more weighted with the heel, and the inside ski lifted sometimes to a notable degree.

One of the most remarkable sights of 1980–1 was Ingemar Stenmark of Sweden skiing the Streiff without once getting into a serious tuck. His 2:13 was ten seconds outside Podborski's winning time, or more than 300 yards at the mile a minute the race averaged. This was one of the steepest courses. The flatter the course the more important the dynamics are. Wengen's length, together with the flats alternating with steeper pitches, puts an especial premium on the retention of the crouch. A Stenmark here would be thirty seconds off the pace. The Swede stated after Kitzbuehel that he would never again ski downhill. Jean-Claude Killy was amongst those strongly criticising him for skiing a downhill and not doing it right. In the US magazine *Ski Racing* he wrote, 'Stenmark was embarrassed by that performance. In fact everyone was embarrassed . . . He is seen as the best technician in the world of skiing today. If skiing is his love and his life, in my opinion he has to try downhill with proper technique, training and attitude.'

The Slaloms

Slalom skiers often protest at the explicit or implicit criticism of their specialism. Slalom, giant and special, singles out the most technically skilful, the skier capable of the swiftest turns, and those with the best psychological attitude to winning. A host of skiers grow up in countries which do not have high enough mountains with sufficiently certain snow cover, or the finance and technical

A sight no one in skiing thought they would see: Stenmark in downhill gear after racing the Streif at Kitzbuehel

organisation, to support downhills. There are many more good special slalom skiers than there are good downhillers. To win in this division is a major triumph.

Asked why he does not dominate special slalom as he does giant slalom, Ingemar Stenmark points to the number of men capable of winning races – the Mahre twins from the USA, Bojan Krizaj of Yugoslavia, the Liechtensteiner, Paul Frommelt, Alexander Zhirov and Vladimir Andreev of Russia, Hans Enn and Christian Orlainsky of Austria. Giant slalom has rather fewer winners, but Stenmark's long supremacy – he won fifteen straight World Cup victories between 1978–9 and 1979–80 – is now under persistent challenge, with Phil Mahre, Zhirov, the Swiss trio of Joel Gaspoz, Jean-Luc Fournier and Jacques Luethy, Bruno Noeckler of Italy, and, when fit, Leonhard Stock of Austria all with the ability to win races.

Giant slalom was a late developer in Alpine skiing. It was first introduced as an Olympic event as late as 1952 and was intended as a compromise between the short sharp turns of special slalom and the much longer, high-speed downhill. Killy was able to win the first World Cup competition in 1967 with a perfect score in all three disciplines, keeping alive the cherished idea, preserved from the twenties, of the all-round skier. But the programme was small – seventeen races as opposed to twenty-eight in 1981–2. It was quickly realised in a more professionalised context that concentrated work on the two slaloms could produce

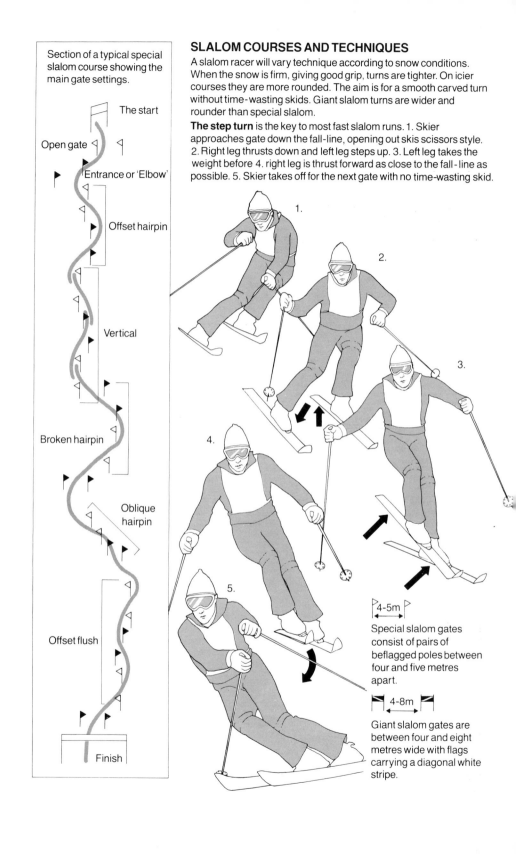

Section of a typical special slalom course showing the main gate settings.

The start

Open gate

Entrance or 'Elbow'

Offset hairpin

Vertical

Broken hairpin

Oblique hairpin

Offset flush

Finish

SLALOM COURSES AND TECHNIQUES

A slalom racer will vary technique according to snow conditions. When the snow is firm, giving good grip, turns are tighter. On icier courses they are more rounded. The aim is for a smooth carved turn without time-wasting skids. Giant slalom turns are wider and rounder than special slalom.

The step turn is the key to most fast slalom runs. 1. Skier approaches gate down the fall-line, opening out skis scissors style. 2. Right leg thrusts down and left leg steps up. 3. Left leg takes the weight before 4. right leg is thrust forward as close to the fall-line as possible. 5. Skier takes off for the next gate with no time-wasting skid.

1.

2.

3.

4.

5.

4-5m

Special slalom gates consist of pairs of beflagged poles between four and five metres apart.

4-8m

Giant slalom gates are between four and eight metres wide with flags carrying a diagonal white stripe.

results that no downhiller, with his week-long slog before his event, could expect to match. Two went into three. One did not. So, after the early domination by the all-rounders, Killy and Austria's Karl Schranz, the slalomers were king.

Gustavo Thoeni of Italy won from 1971 to 1973, Piero Gros, also Italian, in 1974, Thoeni again in 1975, and Stenmark in the next three successive years before Peter Luescher in 1979 and Andreas Wenzel in 1980.

Special slalom has a spicy antiquity. For 10,000 years man skied on skis three metres, or nearly ten feet, long. They were pointed, heavy planks fixed only by a toe strap. They were barely controllable, and certainly not at speed. Sondre Auversen Norheim, from Morgedal in the central area of the mutton chop of Norway, changed all that. A lazy, dreamy carpenter, more out of work than in and supported frequently by his wife's needlework, he chiselled away with home-made plane, adze, saw and chisel at a new kind of ski. On 8 February 1868, a man of forty-three in rough country clothes, he appeared among the gentlemen of Christiania (subsequently renamed Oslo) at their annual ski championships at Iverslokka, and to their consternation won all four competitions – style, jumping, loipe (loop) and free running. Like the carpenter of Reigate who fashioned a cricket bat wider than the wicket, he had begun a revolution. But where cricket restricted the bat width and introduced a third stump for the wicket, skiing went the other way. It saw the advantages of a ski shaped for the job and of a heel binding which rendered control of the ski for the whole of its length. This, in short, was what Norheim achieved. From all his chipping came a ski of 2.4 metres, which was fully sixty centimetres, or two feet, shorter than the clumsy skis of his time. Just as important, he waisted the ski to 69 millimetres from the 84 mm at the shovel in front to 76 mm at the tail. They are measures little changed today. All the same, Norheim would not have achieved his victories at Iverslokka without a further device, the securing of the heel, which gave him the essential control of his new-model skis. This he contrived with twisted osiers, the precursor of the modern ski binding.

The gentlemen of Christiania skied on flat blades, holding a long stout pole which they jabbed in the snow to stop, check or turn around. Their heels flopped up and down and their control of the skis was minimal. Auverson's skis ran straight and true. The newspaper, *Aflenblad*, wrote at the time, 'With a short stick in one hand, which he used rather like a walking stick, and his hat in the other, he starts his free run at a very great speed, making a number of small jumps, each about two or three ski lengths clear of the snow, landing each time with the grace of a dancer and in perfect balance. Until you have seen this man, now 43, ski, you have not seen skiing.'

Like so many pioneers, Norheim never saw the benefit of his ideas. When he returned to Oslo in 1870 the competition was cancelled because of lack of snow. He started a ski factory but it failed and Auverson ('son of a carpenter', for that was his true name, the Norheim coming from the tiny hamlet that sponsored his single expedition) disappeared to America and an unknown grave. All that

remains is a slim granite memorial at Morgedal, Norway. It says 'Sondre Auverson Norheim – Father of Modern Skiing'.

Scandinavians in general were sceptical of innovation, and it was another eccentric, the Austrian Mathias Zdarsky, who saw the natural consequences of fixed-heel skiing and its suitability for much steeper Alpine terrain. Zdarsky, survivor of a First World War avalanche in which he suffered over seventy fractures and dislocations, discovered techniques for descending steep slopes in a series of traverses, curves and turns. It involved basically a heel push and, in German, a 'beinspieltechnik', or leg play. Snow, to Zdarsky, was not a wolf in sheep's clothing, it was a tiger, never fully mastered, but 'beinspieltechnik' helped. To improve technique for it, Zdarsky used poles on the hillside as turning points and called the exercise a torlauf. It is a term still used to describe a slalom in parts of Austria.

Racing, however, was not an end in itself to Zdarsky, and the pursuit of this came most ardently from Arnold Lunn. His father, Henry, had invented the modern winter sports travel trade literally by act of God. A Methodist missionary invalided home from India, in 1892 he organised a conference in Grindelwald, in central Switzerland, aimed at helping to reunite a divided Christendom. At the end of the conference he found himself £500 in pocket, and from there founded a travel business. Since it was 'not done' for the English to go abroad in commercial groups, he founded the Public Schools Alpine Sports Club, booking hotels at a discount rate and passing on some of the benefits to clients under a good clubby cover. In 1903, to amuse his guests, for whom tobogganing and ice skating were as popular as skiing, he organised a cup competition on combined results of all three sports. For the skiing, the Swiss course-setter stuck four poles in a flat field and invited competitors to walk round them. He reasoned that British skiers were neither fit enough nor sufficiently proficient on skis to go either up or down.

The race won by Cecil Hopkinson at Crans-Montana in 1911 was considerably more arduous, but was marked by the same enterprise from Henry Lunn. He persuaded Lord Roberts of Kandahar, a veteran of the Afghan wars, to put up a cup for the event. Lord Roberts was a non-skier but his name and his vice-president's subscription were helpful. Arnold, although himself unable to compete because of a mountaineering accident which had left him with one leg three inches shorter, adopted the name Kandahar when he started up a race club in Mürren to experiment with different ideas and push for the recognition of downhill and slalom racing by FIS. He liked downhill as a test of nerve and stamina but discarded the idea of marking for style as even the Alpine countries were still doing. His answer to the need for a competition testing skill and technique was pairs of flags, known as gates, set down the mountainside in figures. He called it slalom, and set the first course on the practice course at Mürren on 21 January 1921. Thus modern slalom was invented, though not until 1930 did it finally squeeze past FIS and the deeply suspicious Scandinavian countries. Lunn organised the first World Championships for downhill and

The master in trouble: but Stenmark uses all his marvellous agility to recover from this mistake at Val d'Isère

slalom racing in 1931 at Mürren, but they were only recognised retrospectively and then with a slap on the knuckles for his precociousness.

The Swiss University Ski Club was a constant ally in all the experimentation. So, in the late twenties, was the Arlberg Ski Club of Hannes Schneider, based on St Anton. Schneider was the great proponent of the stem christiania turn – one ski pushed out in a fan-like style, the weight transferred to it, and the other ski slid alongside so that the skis were parallel at the completion of the turn. This, in the twenties and thirties, was revolutionary but it proved enduring. Many were still racing the Cortina Olympic slaloms of 1956 with this turn, and in certain circumstances Stenmark does not scorn it today.

The first international ski race was a union of the ideas and spirit of Lunn and Schneider. In the Arlberg–Kandahar races of 1928 at St Anton the racer's finish in downhill conditioned the start number in slalom. It was a criterion which persisted until Italy's slalom specialists, principally Gustavo Thoeni, started to dominate World Cup in the 1970s. In the innocent days of 1929, specialism and financial reward were blissfully absent. While David Zogg from Arosa was winning the men's downhill, the women's winner was Audrey Sale-Barker of the Kandahar Club. A contemporary wrote, 'Audrey Sale-Barker was very tall, ex-

Paul Frommelt of Liechtenstein: winner at Oberstaufen, one of the few specialists in only one discipline, special slalom

tremely slim . . . with pale honey-coloured hair, a vague, dreamy expression, and when she skied I can only describe her as a sleepwalker. She stood very erect with both arms slightly lifted in front of her. She had little or no reserve strength in a race, gave everything she had and often collapsed and fainted when a race was over . . .' In the 1931 Arlberg–Kandahar in Mürren she won everything – slalom, downhill and, of course, combination. Innocence disappeared after the Anschluss of 1937. Lunn secured the release of Schneider from a concentration camp and a sanctuary in the USA on the promise to the Nazis that he would consider keeping the Arlberg–Kandahar at St Anton. Once Schneider was safe he considered the matter again and switched the race to Mürren, to the Nazis' fury.

The thirties saw revolutionary changes which were not to attain their greatest effect until after the war. The first draglifts opened the way to the recreational boom and a mass skiing public. What happened off the snow was as important as what happened on it. Franz Kneissel's Tyrolean woodcarvers in 1936 produced the Splitkein, eighteen wooden lamina glued together for a ski with greater strength and resilience than ever before. By 1956 and the first major televised Winter Olympics, Toni Sailer's hip-wiggling *wedeln* style was supreme. The Kitzbueheler took gold medals in both slaloms and the downhill. He was a gifted athlete, an accomplished golfer and tennis player, a winner at almost everything he attempted. But he had the best skis of their time, and the slalom technique to

utilise them. He turned on flat skis with the minimum of edging, contra-rotating as kids everywhere were doing as rock and roll and the twist took over the dance floors. Killy introduced 'avalement' to slalom, the apparent sit-back style by which he jetted out of turns. He was again helped by a new web-wrap design which gave better properties along the length of the ski. His sit-back was an illusion: his body weight was essentially central over his skis, though not to the degree that Stenmark eventually achieved, as Killy was the first to remark.

Thoeni was more of an all-round skier than he is often given credit for. He competed regularly in downhill – rather more, indeed, than Phil Mahre in 1980–1. In his prime he would have been a regular winner of 'combineds'. These were introduced in the late seventies, primarily to combat Stenmark's dominance, or at least to encourage his participation in downhill. Thoeni was the master of a new sort of turn, the step turn, which all racers now employ – some, like Stenmark, to even greater effect. Where all previous skiing canons demanded weight on the outside ski when approaching a gate and a turn, Thoeni found he could ski a steeper, faster approach by keeping his weight on his inside ski, the one nearer to the gate, until, at the precise moment, he bounced off the inside ski with a stepping-up motion on to the outside ski. With the outside ski he then carved a turn of whatever radius he needed.

Special slalom

A special slalom is decided by two runs on different courses, usually on adjacent slopes, taking place one after the other on the same day with the lowest aggregate time giving the winner. The ideal course allows maximum speed with neat execution and precision but without acrobatics. It must be raced on snow that is as hard as possible; if snow falls during the race it may be removed or stamped in.

A course consists of 55–75 'gates', each of two plastic poles set 1.8 metres (5 ft 11 in.) above the snow on a vertical drop of 180–220 metres (590–720 ft) for men, and 45–60 gates on a vertical drop of 130–180 metres (425–590 ft) for women. At least a quarter of the course must exceed a gradient of 30 degrees, which means the average course length for men is about 550 metres, or a third of a mile, and for women 460 metres. The poles of each gate must be either red or blue, the colours alternating down a course to give guidance to the racer. A slalom gate is between four and five metres (13 ft and 16 ft 3 in.) wide, and, as with all Alpine events, the racer must pass through an imaginary line across the gate with both feet. He is allowed to finish the race on one ski.

There are four main types of gates and combinations – the open and closed gate, the vertical combination and hairpin. The open gate is set against the fall-line (the steepest, most direct line below a skier at any given point), and the closed gate down it. They are used alternately, or in sets, to test not only every radius of turn but also speed in the occasional short traverse (skiing across a slope with a

slight to moderate drop). There must be at least two vertical combinations and four hairpins in every slalom. A skier missing a gate is disqualified and should not continue through further gates. At major events the rules call for videotaping, and a racer may claim a re-run if a gatekeeper blunders (there is one gatekeeper for four gates), or if he is obstructed by a spectator or animal. The run may be provisional until the appeal is checked out.

Racers may inspect the course, walking up through the gates with their skis on, but cannot ski down the prepared course. At least two forerunners are required to ski the course at racing speed. The starter must give a warning in one of three languages – 'Ready' – 'Attention' – 'Achtung'. A few seconds later comes the start signal – 'Go!' – 'Partez!' – 'Los!'

The racers are divided into groups of fifteen according to their latest FIS handicap rankings. The first fifteen are subject to a draw on the eve of the race. In World Cup there is then a sub-group for those with 75 points or more in either downhill or giant slalom. This is to give all-round skiers the chance of a less rutted course. Subsequent racers take part according to their exact FIS ranking, subject to a rule that no nation can have more than four runners in the first or second groups of fifteen. On the second run, the fastest five will depart in reverse order, fifth fastest first and first fastest fifth. This assumes the course will be at its best after about seven runners (including the usual three forerunners).

Special slalom is a set of quick turns, left, right, left, right, passing close to the inside flag but not by the extra few millimetres which mean a hooked ski or bad check. Some racers hit the inside pole so hard with their shoulder that poles are uprooted like matchsticks, but modern plastic poles give to such a degree that time need not be lost. All wear suits with padded knees, elbows and shoulders to prevent bruising.

Special slalom is a test of speed, turning, timing, technique and tactics. The jump start must be perfectly timed. Each run will be accomplished by a top performer at about 23 mph, with victory by tenths or hundredths of a second. Some, like Stenmark, win by hundredths where some enduringly lose by the same eye-blinking margins. No skier ever sets out to ski a certain time, even on a second run where he can easily calculate his needs. He skis to a general objective. Sometimes, where he has nothing to lose after a poorish first run, it will be flat out, on the edge of disaster. Mostly the top slalomers have learned their limits. No one wins who falls. They know that a well-constructed run will keep them in contention. They leave the overstraining to those seeking to displace them. But not always and not inevitably. Like everyone else, they wake up to good days and bad days, and sometimes they ski well on a bad day and less well on a good. Then it may be a question of whether they are mentally strong. Many a skier has won a race having been up all night with a sick stomach or a howling dog.

It is essential that the racer takes the first four gates well. These are set to give him rhythm and only in rare instances – Garmisch for the 1978 World Cham-

Mahre's nest for Stenmark: Steve, *above*, took third place at Aspen. Phil was first with the Swede sandwiched between

pionships was one – are they followed by a savage trap. It is important, though, to take them 'high' – that is, starting them early and above the inside pole of the gate. Trickier hairpins and vertical combinations usually come towards the middle of courses; the last gates should be open and encourage a strong finish. The aim is for a smooth, carved turn through each gate at maximum speed rather than a breakneck attack on each gate and a screaming, scrambling turn which will only lose time in the end. The major part of the turn should be above the gate. The skid has to be avoided at all costs. All racers must study and memorise a course. Most will be seen beforehand, eyes closed, hand pursuing a sinuous line as they mentally rehearse the race. Mentally a racer has to be two or three gates ahead. Conversely, a fall or missed gate nearly always has its origin in a bad mistake two or three gates earlier.

Giant slalom

Giant slalom, like special slalom, consists of two runs, but in major competition they take place on successive days over much longer courses and make greater use of the width of the slopes on which they are set. Although conceived originally as a series of traverses across the fall-line, with more varied turns than the special slalom, the GS in recent years has become more a glorified slalom with many

THE SKI

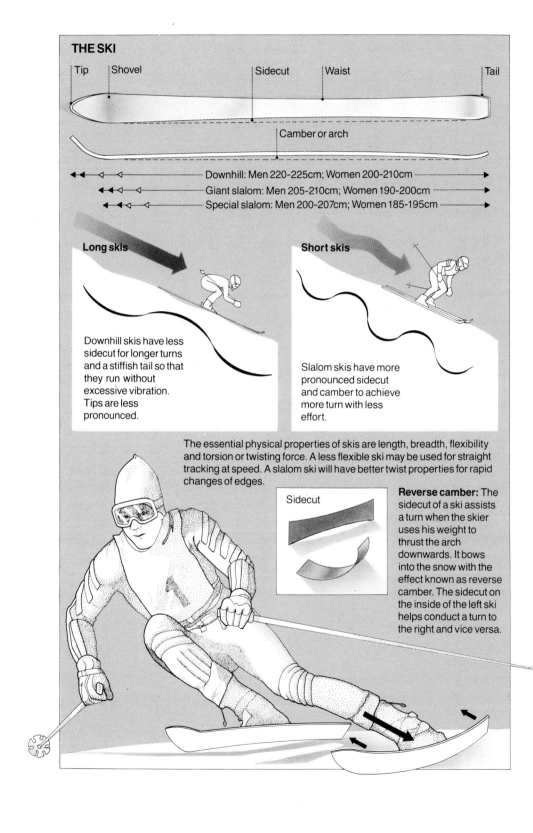

Tip Shovel Sidecut Waist Tail

Camber or arch

Downhill: Men 220-225cm; Women 200-210cm
Giant slalom: Men 205-210cm; Women 190-200cm
Special slalom: Men 200-207cm; Women 185-195cm

Long skis

Downhill skis have less sidecut for longer turns and a stiffish tail so that they run without excessive vibration. Tips are less pronounced.

Short skis

Slalom skis have more pronounced sidecut and camber to achieve more turn with less effort.

The essential physical properties of skis are length, breadth, flexibility and torsion or twisting force. A less flexible ski may be used for straight tracking at speed. A slalom ski will have better twist properties for rapid changes of edges.

Sidecut

Reverse camber: The sidecut of a ski assists a turn when the skier uses his weight to thrust the arch downwards. It bows into the snow with the effect known as reverse camber. The sidecut on the inside of the left ski helps conduct a turn to the right and vice versa.

gates set near the fall-line. FIS are trying to encourage course-setting closer in style to downhill and farther from special slalom, and experiments are taking place in 1981–2 with single races of two kilometres with a 500- to 600-metre vertical drop, and more varied terrain including two jumps.

In World Cup and the World Championships existing rules still apply, with the length about 1300 metres (or four-fifths of a mile), and the vertical drop 300–400 metres (925–1312 ft) for men and 300–350 metres (925–1150 ft) for women. The number of gates must be 15 per cent of the vertical drop, plus or minus five gates, which means that on the World Cup course at Val d'Isère the length is 1291 metres, the drop 398 metres, the average slope 22 degrees (although the steepest will be as much as 50 per cent), and the gates between 55 and 65.

The course should be at least 30 metres (98 ft) wide, half as much again as downhill, and providing for traverses. Further regulations are aimed at keeping the course more open. Thus gates, alternately red and blue, the flags carrying a diagonal white stripe, must be between four and eight metres wide (13–26 ft) and the distance between the inside poles of two successive gates not less than ten metres (33 ft). Gates must not be set down the vertical line of a slope and FIS demands more skilful exploitation of the ground than for special slalom, with single gates encouraged and minimum use of elbows or hairpins.

No training is allowed on the day of the race. Competitors are allowed to study the course – which must be set at least one hour before the start – by climbing alongside on skis or slowly sliding down alongside. Skiing through a gate or practising turns parallel with the course of gates will lead to disqualification.

Giant slalom rules were changed in 1978. By reducing the number of gates, FIS expected to make turns wider, lengthen traverses between the controls and increase average speed. In all of this they succeeded, except in their main aim of benefiting downhillers. Ingemar Stenmark, the slalom specialist, did not lose another giant slalom for two years. He switched to a longer ski which proved faster over soft snow, a matter of some importance since his chief successes to this point were on icier courses. Then he perfected the wide, round giant slalom turns in special training before the season began in Val d'Isère.

The essence of the GS is to find the straightest line through the gates and make as few skidding turns as possible. If a snow plume is thrown up behind the ski, that suggests a good carved turn. A snow plume at the side is bad news. Almost certainly it means a skid, a loss of line, a loss of time and possibly defeat in the race. In GS, as in most skiing, the steepest way down is the fastest. A racer will approach a gate trying to stay as close to the fall-line as the traverse will allow without completely missing the gate. He will use two main types of turn – the step and what is sometimes termed the scissor. As he approaches the inside pole of the gate he will decide instinctively between the two. The step is a more obvious lateral spring from the downhill, or inside, ski to the outside ski, made just before the gate. The skis go into reverse camber, banana-ing into the snow, and the racer

Carved turn: Stenmark is perfectly poised at this slalom gate

glides round on the inside edges as if on a railroad, his right shoulder leading on a right turn, left shoulder forward on a left, literally showing his back to the gate. Both hands will be far forward; his torso, bent like an inverted comma, will have his inside haunch almost scraping the snow as his legs and skis swing round centrifugally.

The scissor, step, or skating, turn is a movement from the downhill to the uphill ski to produce a banked turn. The turn is used by Stenmark, Andreas Wenzel and Phil Mahre in steeper, harder sections of the course where the approach speed may be 40 mph. The step is carried out with varying force. The skier glides on to his uphill ski with a lowering, or sitting back, of his body which unweights his skis. He appears to sit back, but in fact it is a downward rather than a backward motion, while his inside ski glides alongside his outside. This 'downweighting',

achieved by the lowering of his body, paradoxically has the effect of taking weight off his skis and enabling him to swivel them round in the direction he wants to go. As body momentum catches up with the angled skis, the inside edges bite into the snow (the banana, or reverse-camber effect again) and carry him round. The expertise of a Stenmark or Mahre is in judging the right fraction of a second to release these complex movements at speed and secure a turn of the exact radius he needs. One turn serves as a platform for the next traverse and the next turn. It requires great concentration, fitness and practice to achieve.

Parallel slalom

The Parallel is a race run simultaneously by two racers down two courses side by side. The winner is the racer with the lowest aggregate time on two runs, after they have switched courses for the second run. The setting of the course, the configuration of the ground and the preparation of the snow are to be as alike as possible. The vertical drop of the courses must be between 80 and 100 metres and there should be between 20 and 30 gates. Each race should be between twenty and twenty-five seconds. Poles and finish banners must be red for the course on the left going down and blue for the other course. The course-setter must ensure the flow is smooth, that there is a variety in curves, which must be pronounced, and that there are rhythm changes. After the last curve-marker each racer must be directed towards adjacent finish lines.

The racers are started by a visual clock and a set of beeps with a countdown for the last five seconds. Three false starts are allowed. The offending racer on the fourth occasion will be disqualified. Since the racers start simultaneously, they are only timed at the finish on the difference. The first racer cutting the finish-beam starts a clock measuring hundredths of a second. He gets 'zero' and the second racer is given a penalty time between zero and the moment he cuts the photo-electric beam on his finish line.

Usually a Parallel slalom is open to thirty-two racers, frequently selected from an earlier classic race. Sixteen pairs are ranged to a formula – first and thirty-second, second and thirty-first and so on to sixteenth and seventeenth. The lower starting number goes down the red course first and the higher number the blue course. For the second run it is reversed.

The first round is followed by a second elimination run with the sixteen qualifiers going according to the start system. Quarter-finals, semi-finals and final follow. Disqualification will arise from a false start, switching courses, disturbing an opponent, voluntarily or not, missing gates or not finishing. From the quarter-finals onwards, a racer not finishing or disqualified on the first run will race the second with a 1.5 sec. penalty. If neither completes each of the two runs properly, they will race a third run.

12

THE MEN'S DOWNHILL COURSES

John Samuel

Downhill racing has become one of the great modern television spectacles. The ten courses of the 1981–2 season will provide some of the most riveting viewing of the year's sport. Each has been carved from the mountainsides to produce the ultimate challenge of daring and skill to the world's great ski-racers. Eight of them are described here with particular emphasis on the key sections, the places a skier must master with total authority or lose his victory chance. They are in order, not of fame or challenge, but of the downhill racer's schedule.

Val d'Isère France
4 December 1981

The Piste Oreiller–Killy, built in 1967, the first year of the World Cup, traditionally has hosted the first downhill of the season. The O–K piste is more challenging technically than bodily, with the first half above the tree-line and the trail relatively wide even through the pines lower down. About a quarter-way down the course is the Collombin Jump, named after the great Swiss downhiller, Roland Collombin, whose career was ended by a fall in which he badly injured his back here. Even with a pre-jump a racer will be thrown twenty metres or more. Three-quarters of the way down comes the Compression, one of the great features of the entire downhill circuit. With the racer at maximum revs on a steep downhill section he suddenly faces a rise. At 80 mph it is like hitting a wall. He is thrown on the back of his skis. His knees must take the strain or buckle, his belly hits his boots, and at the same time he must set up for the S-turns which immediately follow. Many a racer has ended in the nets here. Many more have lost a second or two which have obliterated their chances of a top-ten place. Val d'Isère is more a technical than a physically intimidating course, but it commands every racer's respect.

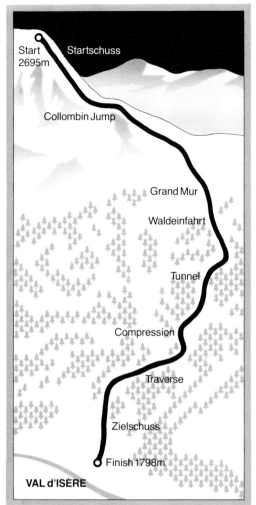

Start 2695m · Startschuss
Collombin Jump
Grand Mur
Waldeinfahrt
Tunnel
Compression
Traverse
Zielschuss
Finish 1798m
VAL d'ISÈRE

Living on the edge: Ken Read hits the Zielschuss at Val d'Isère at maximum speed. He finished second

Val Gardena Italy
13 December

Val Gardena in the Dolomites is the 1972 World Championship course, steadily growing in racers' estimation and with a ready identity under the sugar-loaf peaks with their reddish hue. It has two main features. The first are the Camel Bumps – three jumps coming rapidly one after the other, and some of the toughest in ski-racing. The first and second are fairly easy, the third is what it is all about – a landing at 75 mph. 'It's like coming up to the White Cliffs of Dover,' says Konrad Bartelski. The final landing is on the flat with rapid deceleration and the body suffering all the shock. The jumps are spread over about eighty metres. The skier leaps twenty metres over the first and skis another fifteen metres. Then he springs

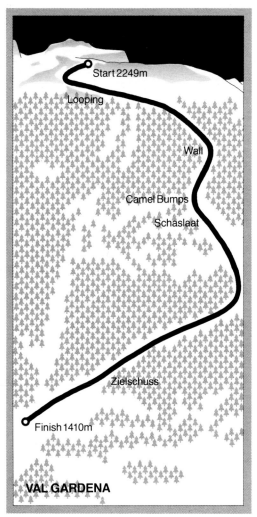

Val Gardena. *Above:* Out of the box.
Opposite: Uli Spiess springs 40 metres
to clear the third Camel jump in 1980

another twenty metres for a 5-metre landing. Then, to keep him busy, there is a final 20-metre jump before hitting the flat. Trouble usually means a crash, and a nasty one at that if the final fall is on the flat. All skiers prefer to tumble on a slope, none more so than camel-hopping downhillers . . . In 1980 Austria's Uli Spiess, winner at Val d'Isère and going for broke here, sprang forty metres off the second hump to overleap the third. He gained up to half a second but lost his advantage to finish fifth to Peter Mueller.

Next after the Camel comes the Schaslaat turns, a bumpy meadow of pure ice sprayed to ensure the course does not break up. It's like a rough, corrugated ice rink with longish turns and bumps which must be executed without the skis washing around and losing precious tenths or hundredths of a second. Every exit must be neat with maximum acceleration.

Morzine France
9 January 1982

Television dramatically curtain-raises the action here with the racers switching from a sidehill on to a traverse which is one of the key sections. The racers must come out high, like divers curving from the top board rather than the middle, with leaps of thirty metres or more. A quick section of S-turns leads into a jump. The racer cannot stay too long on his edges or stand up too much and catch the wind. The flatter he keeps his skis through this part the faster he will be. A downhiller is not looking for style marks here. Klammer in his prime would let his skis run early through such sections. His body position might look radical, his skis were running fast. Weirather and Podborski have learned from Klammer. Like

him, they let their skis go early, but their upper bodies will be quieter, finishing turns quickly and getting back into the tuck. Less spectacular, but an evolution in downhill technique.

Kitzbuehel Austria

16 January

Above the ancient walled village of Kitzbuehel in the eastern Tyrol the Streif course for the Hahnenkamm trophy hosts the major downhill of Alpine skiing. It is what Wimbledon is to tennis and St Andrews to golf. As a course it has everything. It can never be won by a fluke.

There are two vital areas among its many tests. The top section is recorded by Austrian TV about a minute before the racer is seen by viewers, and it shows him in one of the key areas, from the Mausfalle (Mousetrap) into the Steilhang (Steep Wall). The race begins abruptly with quick, icy turns taking the racer directly into the fall-line. A left turn must be negotiated as close as possible to the gate before the sheer ledge of the Mausfalle. The slightest error before the jump and the skier may be thrown forty metres. Even after a pre-jump or leg retraction he will probably jump twenty-five metres. He lands on a steep pitch but quickly the course tries to snare him with a sudden 'flat' with grinding deceleration followed by a sharp left turn leading to the Steilhang. The icy convex slope of the Steilhang turns on to a narrow, flat, tree-lined path known as the Alte Schneise. When he starts the Steilhang the racer cannot see the exit. The curvature is forcing him lower and lower towards the trees, guarded here by an enormous fence of intertwined saplings and hay. His speed, around 70 mph, in combination with the ice is luring him towards disaster at the 'Bamboo Curtain', the dramatic safety fence here. But he has to exit at maximum pace on a perfect line to stand a chance of winning, for the Alte Schneise lasts nearly fifty seconds of the race and must be taken well.

A left and right mark the entry to the Hausberg section, named after the small house on the edge of the course where spectators and cameramen perch on the roof for a view of the next test, a difficult right-hander followed instantly by a jump known as the Hausbergkante. The racer lands in a slight compression and at the same time he must prepare for a left punctuated by another jump. The finish of the turn is a rough, icy, fall-away traverse which must be completed on the strictest line, high and in a good aerodynamic position, so that the finish switchback can be carried. This section, the Zielschuss, provides spectators at the finish with one of the greatest spectacles in sport as the racer swoops like a fly on a wall, appearing and disappearing while the crowd holds its breath in suspense to see whether the agonised muscles can hold on and he will crest the final knoll. His body is tired, the racer has had to fight every millimetre all the way down, the light can be poor, the track is bumpy. The last dregs of concentration and fitness

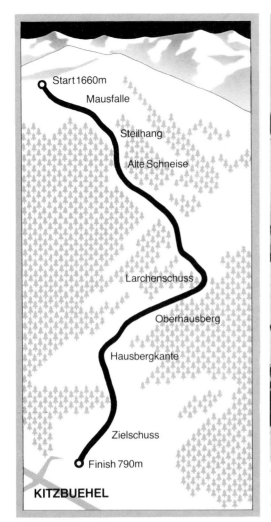

Start 1660m
Mausfalle
Steilhang
Alte Schneise

Larchenschuss

Oberhausberg

Hausbergkante

Zielschuss

Finish 790m

KITZBUEHEL

The Zielschuss at Kitzbuehel: the racer appears and disappears, while the crowd holds its breath in suspense

are being drained here, and no one present can miss the drama and tension before the downhiller flashes under the finish banner.

Wengen Switzerland

23 January

Wengen, in the Bernese Oberland, is the cockpit of the most spectacular scenery of all Switzerland. The Lauberhorn, the race which it hosts, is the longest and oldest race in Swiss racing history, and vies with the Hahnenkamm in prestige and significance. Wengen, accessible only by one of the oldest rack and pinion railways in Switzerland, sits on a sunny plateau beneath a range of mountains

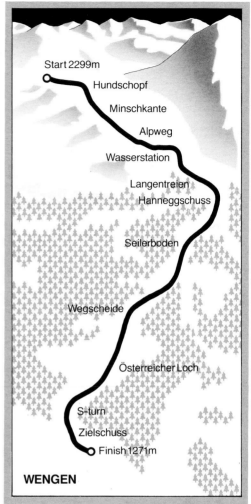

Start 2299m
Hundschopf
Minschkante
Alpweg
Wasserstation
Langentreien
Hanneggschuss
Seilerboden
Wegscheide
Österreicher Loch
S-turn
Zielschuss
Finish 1271m

WENGEN

Above: All-out on the longest: Switzerland's own Toni Buergler en route for victory on the 4.29-kilometre Lauberhorn course at Wengen. *Opposite:* The Hundschopf at Wengen: one of the trickiest sections, a hard right and a left following a long, rolling meadow

which are part of climbing lore – the Jungfrau, Eiger, Schreckhorn, Wetterhorn and Mönch. It is one of three neighbouring resorts – Grindelwald and Mürren are the others – where the English pioneers joined with the Swiss to evolve Alpine ski-racing. Sir Arnold Lunn, the inventor of the slalom on the slopes of the Schiltgrat above Mürren, celebrated his eightieth birthday by climbing the Lauberhorn mountain and skiing down the run which takes its name.

The course is 4.29 kilometres with a vertical drop of 1028 metres. The top of the course is over a long, rolling meadow into hard right and left turns known as the Hundschopf. This section is videoed and introduced when the racer is thirty or forty seconds further down the course. The next critical point is the Minschkante, a steep pitch ending in a compression where the racer must take a sharp right turn. His exit here determines his speed for the entire middle section of the

course. For about forty seconds the racer tries to maintain speed over a small bridge across a stream, through a railway tunnel and across another bridge under which holiday skiers cross the course. After the Hanneggschuss, a narrow, steep section through trees, the piste then hits the Österreicher Loch (Austrian Hole), a sharp compression where a set of Austrians once fell to give it its name.

The make-or-break section for the fastest skiers comes at the finish S. After two minutes' hard racing their legs are burning, their concentration under the fiercest challenge. Now at 80 mph comes this narrow, icy, left-right-left section where the racer is setting up blindly, choosing his carved line from his knowledge of the course, each turn banked so that it opposes rather than assists the exit. Turning 'off camber' at this speed means the most exact of ski edge sets in the rattling ice. The whole passage only lasts five or six seconds but a racer can easily

lose or make more than half a second. Half-way through the last turn the trail falls away towards the drop-off for the Zielschuss, or finish straight. Cameras and spectators set up here for one of the most spectacular finishes in racing, as the skier appears like Batman. Unless he is exactly poised the racer will be in trouble, as was Peter Mueller in 1981. If he jumps too far it is a flat landing on tired legs. Mueller sat back on his skis and zipped straight into a fence, dislocating a shoulder and ruining his chance of a third World Cup downhill title. Little wonder that no racer can be said to be a world-beater until he has won Wengen.

Schladming Austria
31 January

World Championship course: Schladming's Planai downhill introduced Klammer to the world, but Canadians have excelled on it

Schladming in 1982 has the distinction of staging the World Championships, held as a separate event every four years, although World Championship medals are awarded with Olympic medals in the intervening years. The Planai downhill course has suffered extreme bad luck with the weather in recent times, and not all is accountable to its relatively low finishing altitude of 758 metres (2237 feet).

Artificial snow-making has been introduced on the finish section for the Championships – the first in Austria. The course of 3.6 kilometres with a vertical drop of 997 metres is steep and fast in good conditions.

A sudden thaw destroyed the World Cup race there in 1981, and in 1979 the event was annulled because of rain and bad visibility after twenty-nine racers had gone (after thirty the race must stand). But it was here with a record time of 1:41.77 that Klammer announced his presence to the world in 1973, and the Canadians have usually done well with Dave Irwin winning in 1975 and Ken Read in 1978.

The first key section is known as Italian Hole, where a group of Italians crashed some years ago. After a series of little jumps it is a set to the left, then a sharp right-hander falling away into trees with a huge net to remind racers of the penalties. The exit must be exact or speed will be lost through the forest section which follows. The final turn into the Zielschuss, a left-hander, must be perfectly carved for the long, steep run-in with a bump just before the finish. The course is not a particularly technical one, but it crosses an access road at a number of points and the road jumps can daunt the less psychologically tough.

Garmisch-Partenkirchen West Germany
13 February

Garmisch and its twin town of Partenkirchen provide an Alpine downhill centre unlike any other. It nestles snugly in the inlets of the South Bavarian plains as they wash against the Alps. Most of the population of 27,000 are elderly, but towards the end of the festival period of Fasching swarms of people of all ages pour in for the World Cup downhill, which provides a feature of the season along with the Bach and Brahms recitals and the Bavarian State Opera.

Garmisch is one of the courses which stages the classic Arlberg–Kandahar meeting on a rotational basis (the others are St Anton and Chamonix), and its 3.32 kilometres, with a vertical drop of 920 metres, demands a technically strong performance from a racer. He has to get into his tuck and stay in it though his thighs burn. He must not lose an inch on the corners. It has no major jump and no compression, but it is still highly regarded by the racers for the tests it does impose under the northern faces of the Zugspitze.

At the top there is a critical section called the Troegelhang with a set of tight, technical turns finishing with this exit which must be taken with maximum speed into a long wooded path. The racer will never get his speed back if he misses it here. The first intermediate time here is not displayed on the television screen, but the crowd on the course will be fully alert to a fast start and their responses will be a good guide to the televiewer. The middle section of Garmisch is what is described by racers as flat, and though this represents a considerable slope even to an advanced recreational skier, it will be much less severe than the pitches. One major feature, the Eishang or ice wall, a convex dome with a sharp right turn at

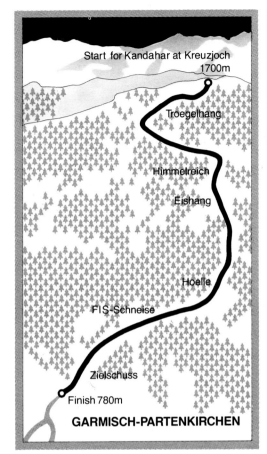

Start for Kandahar at Kreuzjoch
1700m

Troegelhang

Himmelreich

Eishang

Hoelle

FIS-Schneise

Zielschuss

Finish 780m

GARMISCH-PARTENKIRCHEN

Opposite: On top of the world: a downhiller's vista of Garmisch. *Above:* Britain's Konrad Bartelski, a veteran at 26, goes for the finish

the bottom, offers a pitch that only a trained athlete would want to take in a direct line. In its prepared icy state it is almost impossible to traverse, so it is closed to holiday skiers immediately after a race until such time as a less treacherous surface forms or is formed.

Aspen Colorado, USA
5 and 6 March

Aspen is a quiet mining town, which fell into decay until, after World War Two, the ski bug tunnelled in, bringing fortunes undreamed of even by the Fortyniners. Set spectacularly on Aspen Mountain, known to regulars as Ajax, it kicks off with the highest start in World Cup – 10,680 feet – where even experienced racers may catch their breath on cold days. Colorado is a thousand miles from any ocean, and famous for its powder snow, so light and moistureless that it can be blown from

The Men's Downhill Courses 109

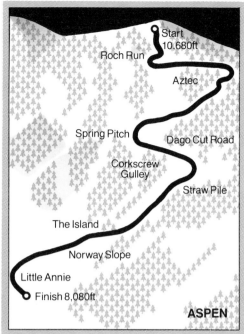

World Cup winner: Harti Weirather masters the second turn at Aspen in the thunderous run which brings him the downhill title

the hand like thistledown. The West, in one or two recent seasons, has suffered snow drought which has caused even Colorado to think in terms of man-made snow, but Aspen's great complex of skiable mountains well justifies its reputation as the USA's ski capital.

Although one of the shortest downhills in World Cup at 3170 metres (1.97 miles), with a vertical drop of 792 metres (2600 feet), Ruthie's Run ruthlessly weeds the good from the outstanding. High as it may be, Aspen's latitude is roughly equivalent to Sicily's and the tree-line is up to the mountain peak. The course, cut through the conifers, begins with a fifty-second flat, a difficult, undulating one, where the racer has to ski rather than glide. Then he soars over a jump and into the Aztec turn, which has a banked wall-of-death exit known as the Aeroplane. It must be made with high precision for a winning time. This was where Harti Weirather and Steve Podborski really fought out the final World Cup races of 1981.

Ruthie's Run for the last third is full of fast, steep, punishing turns. Spring Pitch has been widened and is a little less steep, but it is a lot faster and the path via Dago Cut Road leads to Straw Pile, which requires a hard right turn in a compression. At the bottom of Little Annie comes another compression followed by the finish schuss. Aspen, in 1982 as in 1981, provides a spectacular finish to the Downhill season.

13

LIVING LIKE A SNOW GYPSY

Konrad Bartelski

The shining peaks sharply dissect the horizon. The white valleys descend into haze, hiding the town of Bolzano. For the moment the reality of schedules and commitments is submerged in the splendour of the Dolomites. I am looking at the top of Europe and my vision is as clear as the sky. Overdrafts, alarm calls and deadlines dissolve among the towering crags.

Soon, though, I am back in the workshop. Red flags trace a colourful line against the clean white snow. Here in the Val Gardena World Cup downhill race we will battle at 80 mph for hundredths of a second. Here we will see the product of our seclusion, hard work and dedication. The specks of colour speeding down the mountainside are racers warming up, turning their minds and bodies for the battle over the shining snow. It will be close, really hard fought – literally no inches given. Risks that cannot be justified will be taken. All help will be shed. The racers will soon be alone, hurtling down with just the brain communicating

Konrad Bartelski has skied for Britain in three Olympic Games, finishing twelfth in the Lake Placid downhill. He was also fifteenth in the 1974 World Championships. Amsterdam-born of a British mother and Polish father, he is one of the most experienced downhillers on the World Cup circuit.

Corvara, Val Gardena. *Above:* Overdrafts and alarm calls disappear among the towering crags. *Top right:* You prepare for complete commitment. *Below right:* You finish off a nice turn early – you come out nice and easy. That's exciting . . .

to the body, at its simplest keeping it from bulging the nets that line the course.

The crowds build up around the trickier sections. My jaw is already tired; my teeth have been subconsciously rotating on my favourite cinnamon chewing gum, vainly trying to dissipate the tension that is building up. The service men from the many different manufacturers are hovering around. The coaches nervously unwrap their second packet of cigarettes. My brain is trying to stay in isolation, focusing only on the course that lies ahead – the jumps that lie so deceivingly still, the bumpy turns where the skis chatter around like sticks on corrugated iron, the compressions that can suck the body into what feels like a brick wall. Every bump and hollow will be navigated as precisely as possible.

The first man explodes out of the box, leaving pure new traces in the snow. The first times are written on a board giving clues to the ride that lies ahead. Is the course faster or slower than practice? Are there parts breaking up? Reports are barked over the different teams' walkie-talkies. The situation has to be carefully analysed. Slowly the artist chooses the colours that he will use for his painting, yet only when the picture is finished will he know if the choice was right.

You are preparing for a complete commitment. The finger-nails reach for the boots, the warm muscles loosely stretch in anticipation of the rigours they will

endure. Colour lenses are fitted into the goggles, the eyes will be wanting to see all that is possible, not fixed in the rigid muscles of anxiety. Fingers are eased into the tight gloves. The boots are fastened under the close scrutiny of a manufacturer's representative, then carefully guided into the bindings, to be finally checked by yet another service man. Skis are cleaned of the last crystals of snow. The lungs are already stretching to grab all the oxygen they can reasonably take at 8000 feet. Calf, thigh, back and stomach muscles are given their last stretches. The last run of the course is traced in the mind. Slowly and carefully the poles are planted in the snow beyond the timing wand, seemingly in contrast to the speed at which body and mind will react over the next two minutes. Anticipation almost sucks the skis through the gates.

A last deep breath and then a peaceful silence. The beeps of the timing clock switch the body on to reflex control. Timing, preparation and determination now take over. The body explodes out of the starting-gate and tranquillity is rudely replaced by the rush of excited motion. The only thought now is 'faster'. The gates, the leaps, the turns, the chattering skis are a tape of sight and sound run through at a speed which almost defies conscious thought.

Your body reacts instinctively to what it has been trained to do through the long hours of practice. Bad runs are disjointed. Good runs are where you are in tune with yourself. Downhill is a pure, clean sport. That is why it is so rewarding, but you do not want blots half-way down the page. You finish off a nice turn early – you come out high and easy. That's exciting you and stimulating you to go on to the next part even better. It's a test in perfection. A bad corner, scratching round, destroys the whole pleasure. Smoothness is all, you cannot have a really good run without it. It is quite unlike other sports, only a motor-racing driver perhaps has the same feel. There'll be one lap when you hardly seem to be changing gear or pushing pedals, hardly braking at all. You'll be at one with the energy all around you, a part of life, a part of infinity. Everything goes so smoothly, and smoothness always leads to a good time.

Through the finish the mind switches back to a slower-motion reality. I search for the scoreboard. One minute, fifty-four seconds and seventy-odd hundredths. The mathematical interpretation mixes with the gut reaction to the run. A small smile breaks out involuntarily. The reactions of people around me confirm that things have not gone too badly. 1.80 seconds behind the winner, Harti Weirather of Austria. Definitely a step, if not two, in the right direction. The satisfaction of a good run makes the agonising steps at the end of a six-mile run in summer training just that much more bearable.

The finish area is a jam of people. There are handshakes for the winner, surrounded by the people who helped him do it and the many more who would like to think they did. After his isolated state on the hill, the winner must adjust to the attention of the press, the sponsors and the spectators. It is a vibrating world, far from the emotional experience he enjoyed on the mountain.

Then the guillotine drops, for winners and losers alike. The steps to the car

Smoothness always leads to a good time: under the banner, and you look straightaway
for the scoreboard

may be slow and heavy with disappointment or smooth and carefree with elation.
The body and brain are now reacting to the highs and lows of intense physical
exposure. The short drive to the hotel allows the mind to re-run the tape – to
analyse the race, the mistakes, the 'close ones', the good turns and the bad. The
four walls of the hotel bedroom finally bring everything back into ordinary focus.
Back to the next destination, the next goal – the race in St Moritz. The tight suit

The finish is a jam of people. It's a vibrating world, far from the isolation of the mountain.
Here Paul Frommelt (*centre*) celebrates his Oberstaufen slalom win flanked by Steve Mahre
(*left*) and Ingemar Stenmark

is peeled off and chucked on to the bed, ready to be squeezed into the suitcase,
open and waiting to be stuffed with this week's collection of dirty clothes. Lunch
is rushed through, the tongue still too numb to appreciate flavours. Sometimes it
is a blessing in disguise – food in the Alps is not all culinary excellence.

The huge bags harbouring the dozen or so pairs of skis carried by each racer are
man-handled into the transit bus. The rest of the bags are thrown in to complete
the jigsaw. The rush of departure sometimes seems faster and more hectic than
the race a few hours earlier. Snow-covered roads and treacherous passes, usually
with one hairpin too many, keep one mindful of risks. A good tape in the cassette
adds a bit of rhythm to the rumble of the burdened engine straining up and down
the steep inclines.

The road stretches ahead in a recognisable pattern. The passes of the Alps are
as familiar as the streets back home. Some members of the team drift off to sleep,
bored with the detail of travel. Others enjoy the scenes that each bend in the road
produces. There is always an interesting house or castle missed on previous
journeys. The strength of a natural fortress surrounds the small group of skiers,
oblivious to the bouncing of the vehicle over the rough roads. The majestic peaks
stand forcefully over the little mini-bus as it nibbles away at the kilometres. The

coach sifts through his 'mickey mouse' money, trying to find the last Italian lire to pay one of the numerous road tolls. Schillings, francs and marks come rolling out. There is a whip round for the remaining coins. Banking hours usually coincide with training times and each country has different opening hours; some small chores require skilful management.

A few kilometres ahead and the sleeping bodies are given a nudge to dive down for their passports. One of the younger members collects a barrage of abuse when he discovers that his is in his bag and buried under a mound of luggage in the back. The dark-blue and gold passports are waved at a sinister-looking customs guard, his eyes widening as they move over our cargo. A handful of stickers makes him happy – can't be any contraband there! A quick wave and we are 'back on the road'.

The cassette collection has been well worked over. The headlights pencil weird designs on the cliffs overhanging the road. We absorb them silently. The darkness and the drone of the engine make us think of a good meal and bed. The hunger pangs seem to put dynamite into the driver's acceleration foot and the corners are getting the James Hunt treatment. Bribing the coach with promises of hot coffee, we manage to grab a few minutes in Innsbruck station for a quick sandwich and a chance to buy an English paper. Only a day old! Our eyes scan the pages for news, football scores or even the gold prices. The paper is quickly dissected into true 'fish and chips' material. Then it is back into the bus. The driver's foot is flat to the floor along the motorway. Somebody mentions the downhill. 'Oh, was that today?' comes a muffled murmur from under one of the jackets.

'St Moritz 35 kilometres.' A blue and white sign flashes like a cactus in the desert. We are actually going to get there. Entering the sleeping village late at night, the next task is to find the race office. One of the boys, half dozing in the back, catches a glimpse of a sign almost hidden behind a bright Christmas tree and saves us an unwanted sightseeing trip around this famous resort.

We are delighted to hear that our request to stay with the US team has been granted. Small teams tend to get small hotels, so we have to develop a few tricks. It's just that a big bath allows you to do a bit of laundry as well. After a year on the circuit, most racers have got their retirement plans sorted out – opening laundrettes in the Alps. The last dregs of energy are used on the unloading of the van. Video batteries, like us, tend to prefer the warmth! The overloaded bedroom, stacked with bags and jackets, suffers a few more. A quick dive into bed and the next thought is lost in the sleep that seemed such a long time coming.

In the breakfast room the next morning the coach greets us with the welcome news that we aren't going up the hill. As visions of having a whole day to ourselves are forming, he quickly reminds us of our schedule. Sort out the ski room, go for a run, gymnastics, watch video of the race.

The first cup of coffee is tentatively raised to my lips – what will it be like this week? Another question is quickly answered as the hot, coloured water runs over my tongue. The new boys on the team ask for the locations of various services:

Living like a Snow Gypsy 117

grocers, paper shop (if there is a decent one), bank, coffee shop. I run off some suggestions, sounding like the Swiss Tourist Office, although it might be more complimentary. The breakfast fried eggs look extremely lonely, lacking the company of some good sausages and bacon. The scraps of the newspaper are distributed around the table as we attempt to get up to date, or rather – out of date! On the fourth croissant I decide I had better get something done and not slide into my habitual 'mañana' state.

One bag is emptied straight into the tub, out comes the address book, the fingers spin around the dial, and suddenly I am home for a few minutes. Hardly any time to take a breath between words, there is so much to report. The counter ticks away, very faintly, in the background – a reminder not to pause too often. I hang up and then remember all I was really going to say. Now it's on to the letters. The brain struggles to put faces to the names and streets. The silence is broken by the shrill of a phone. The Yanks are having a game of soccer at four this afternoon. 'Want to join us?' 'Where?' I ask. 'Outside the front of the station.' It's not Wembley . . . but who cares?

So, quickly, the day is eaten away. An evening meal and time for early bed. A tasteless picture hangs squint on the facing wall. The bed is too soft. My mind drifts, as it so often does, on to the race in four days' time. The course unrolls in the smoothest of ribbons. Sleep gently descends.

14

THE PLAID AND THE PLASTIC
The Scottish and English Scene

Alan Smith

Scotland is the natural breeding ground for British ski-racers, but the 1980-1 season emphasised the beneficial effects to be gained from Alpine, and in particular Austrian, 'finishing schools'. Not the expensive, upper-crust establishments that phrase conjures up, but schools which carry a full educational syllabus and in addition a comprehensive skiing, and ski-racing, training.

Martin Bell, who at sixteen added the British senior title to the junior one he had taken three times, had, at the time of his success in Val d'Isère, been at school in Stams for a year and a half, while Kirstin Cairns, who so nearly took the women's senior championship and did win the downhill, spent four years at Schladming.

Britain's ski teams took on a new look in this, the post-Olympic season, with only Konrad Bartelski remaining of the old guard, and most of the others five to ten years his junior. When Konrad, then twenty-five, finished twelfth in Lake Placid he was putting up the best performance ever by a British male skier in an Olympic downhill, and during the summer he went to New Zealand and there beat Ken Read, the Canadian who had been favourite for the Olympic race.

Bartelski, who has himself lived in Austria for several years, though now London-based, started the 1980-1 season with placings in the teens, which augured well for the next couple of months, but instead of making the hoped-for progress into the leading group his form deteriorated. His runs, like the curate's egg, were 'good in parts', but he could not get it all together.

He missed the British championships in favour of the World Cup scene, leaving the field open to the younger element. Freddie Burton, five years younger, was the senior member of the team there. In terms of experience Burton, a student at Marseilles University, has little over most of his teammates.

Martin Bell is the son of an RAF instructor and his mother teaches French at a school near Edinburgh, so it is not surprising that both physically and mentally he is mature for his age. His precocious skiing talent, which won him the three national junior titles and the chance to study in Austria, seems on the evidence of

Britons in the snow: men's team members David Mercer, Paul Hourmont, Frederick Burton, John Clark, Martin Bell, and trainer Ernst Zwinger

his first season to have made a successful transition to senior racing, which is by no means universal among young skiers. He showed up well in the appalling conditions for the Lowlanders Championships in Val d'Isère, when training was interrupted by blizzards, and the downhill races for both men and women, as well as the men's slalom which had to be squeezed into the same day, were run in frost-biting temperatures. Bell clocked the best time in the final training run, but in the race proper was fourth to the experienced Dutchman, Peter van der Swaluw, combined Lowlander champion in 1979 and 1980. France's Jean Martinal, on the fringe of World Cup class, was equalled for second place by Welshman Ivan Jones, a member of the British Citadin team, the surprise result of the meeting.

Bell and Burton, close behind in fourth and fifth, were supported by Matt Cooper and Paul Hourmont in the team which was attempting to win the men's Lowlander Championship for a second year running. At that stage the Dutch were, as usual, in close contention, but with both the van der Swaluw brothers falling in the slalom, and Burton and Bell again fourth and fifth – but in reverse order – the title, and the *Daily Telegraph* salvers that go with it, were theirs.

Kirstin Cairns finished third to Holland's Katusha Esser – who with sister Linda, now Mrs Stricker, has a cupboardful of Lowlander Trophies – and Hetty of the ubiquitous van der Swaluw family, in the women's downhill, and fell in the slalom, but this race provided one of the bravest victories of the season. Felicity

British women racers: Ingrid Grant, Lesley Beck, Moira Langmuir, Kirstin Cairns and Clare Booth

Blyth, 17, better known as 'Flic', whose family is to Scottish skiing almost what the van der Swaluws are to Dutch, had spent much of the lead-up time to the downhill making sure that other members of her team survived the Arctic conditions, not realising that her own feet were suffering from frostbite. She raced the Lowlander slalom and, with no feeling in her feet, produced a superb second run to beat Katusha Esser, but by the next day her feet were so swollen and painful she could not even put her boots on, let alone ski, and had to be sent back to Scotland for treatment. Luckily it proved less drastic than it might have, and she will be back with the British team for the 1981–2 season.

Usually the British championships, when they are in Val d'Isère, are held before the Lowlanders, but this time they came after. Bell decidedly reversed Lowlander placings with Martinal, who comes from Val d'Isère, in the downhill and then held off Burton in the slalom after Burton had led him on the first run. Rivalry among the team, and especially these two, by keeping them at full stretch, will surely act to the benefit of them all, as the Austrians and, in their heyday, the French have also found.

Kirstin Cairns was also an easy winner of her downhill, and was odds on to clinch the overall title on her eighteenth birthday, only to catch a ski tip eight gates from the end of the first run and fall out. The race resulted in that rarity, a dead-heat, between Moira Langmuir, who had been third in the downhill, and

Anne Robb, who had been in the Lake Placid Olympic team and has now retired from serious racing to open a sportswear shop in Aberdeen. She never has raced downhill, so the overall title went to Moira, 18, from Edinburgh.

Scotland in general, and Edinburgh especially, with its splendid Hillend artificial slope, may provide the nucleus of Britain's skiing future, but cannot lay claim to one of the brightest of the younger racers, Andrea Jochum, who even next season will still only be in the junior team. Andrea, from Niederau, Austria, where her father is a ski instructor – her mother is British – was only fifteen when she made a heroic and so nearly successful effort to land the Martini–Kandahar slalom in Courmayeur, against skiers some a decade or more her senior.

Valentina Iliffe, who retired after Lake Placid after an unhappy final couple of seasons, finished first in the M-K slalom and giant slalom in 1980, but as these races are for Citadin skiers – those from towns and cities not in themselves ski centres – Bardonecchia-based Valentina was ineligible for the prizes, and so was Andrea. But this did not detract from her fine effort, which pulled her up from fifth after the first run in difficult conditions to finish behind Germany's Andrea Hoffmann.

Since Fraser Clyde, an ex-racer whose father Bob is overlord of Cairngorm (he runs the chairlift company there, lifeline of the region as far as skiers are concerned), was appointed Alpine Director by the National Ski Federation a year or so ago, a more positive, more ambitious approach is discernible. The 'didn't he/she do well' attitude to someone who has just reached the top fifty in an international race is, thankfully, not as prevalent as it was. Perhaps Valentina Iliffe's great disadvantage was that, in her early days, she was 'protected' by being only third string to two of the best skiers this country has ever produced, Gina Hathorn and Divina Galica. Now, with the exception of Konrad Bartelski, the youngsters are in the firing line and, although some, maybe many, will fail to make the grade, those that do should be tougher and more experienced than British skiers of their age have been in the past.

Scotland will inevitably have the biggest part to play, both as a source of skiing talent and as a venue for races of increasing importance. The British championships, now international, are due to return there in the coming season, and in 1982–3 it is intended to hold the Europa Cup final at Aviemore.

The British Federation had their first experience of organising a Europa Cup race last December at Crans-Montana, Switzerland, with Remy Martin as the sponsors. The French firm announced in September 1980 that they were putting £75,000 into British skiing over the two subsequent seasons, part towards the costs of the British teams and part towards the running of the Europa Cup races, culminating in the final in Scotland.

It was in Crans-Montana, in 1911, that the British organised the first international downhill, but the local weather gods clearly did not feel that that gave them any particular pull, and the races had to be postponed for five days because of lack of snow. When they were run the races, downhill and giant slalom for

Britain's plastic scene: preparing for a Thomson Trophy race on the Gloucester slope

women, brought no great encouragement for the British competitors. Kirstin Cairns, who had been only two seconds off the best training times, finished some ten seconds behind the downhill winner, Gabi Weber of Austria.

Lack of snow was a widespread disease throughout Europe last season. Scotland had one of its least active seasons for many years right up to the bitter end, with the cancellation of the British Universities championships in April with the thinnest covering of snow since the meeting was first held in 1965. But how much better off was Schladming, where for the third successive year the men's downhill was 'rained off'? Weather conditions are something skiers just have to accept, and they can be good in Scotland, as at the first National Championships in 1967, when spectators were in shirt-sleeves.

Bell and Burton both performed exceptionally well when the British top squad went to the Southern Hemisphere during the summer. In two international downhills in New Zealand they both finished ahead of Konrad Bartelski – Burton finishing tenth and seventh and Bell eleventh and fourteenth. Then they went on to Australia where, in August, Bell won the Australian slalom championship at Thredbo, NSW. Both skiers are now qualified for World Cup downhill.

Early in 1981 Peter Stuyvesant announced a massive, and comprehensive, sponsorship for sport, amounting in all to around £500,000 and taking in bobbing, water-skiing and wind-surfing as well as snow skiing. Skiing is to get some £90,000 a year, part of which goes to help the British team. The remainder is aimed at raising the general standard of skiing in Britain and giving the true amateur competitions to aim at and carrying prizes worth £500 for the man and woman champion, reached through a series of regional qualifiers.

15

SKI JUMPING

Ron Pickering

When I stand at the top of the tower looking down the in-run, let alone to the abyss beyond, I cannot comprehend how the ski jumper makes his first uncompromising move. The drama of the event is mind-blowing. Here are young men, often in their teens, launching themselves from a platform at speeds of up to 75 mph at which it would be fatal simply to fall. Having taken off with as much vertical lift as possible, they defy the pull of gravity for as long as wingless humans can, before landing the length of a football pitch away. In their attempts they are actually flying, rather than falling, using their body and their skis as a flat parachute to delay their descent, but at the same time leaning forward to cut down wind resistance in the horizontal plane. Casual observers may think it absurd for judges to demand more from competitors than the courage and skill to produce distance. In fact they give style marks for calmness, precision and control, and they are absolutely right, for only then can the risks be justified. Like gymnastics and diving, there is a marvellous aesthetic quality to the sport, and it is built into the rules.

Competitions take place on two different types of hills, one called a 70-metre, the other a 90-metre. There is another sport called Ski Flying, not included in the Olympic Games or World Championships, but controlled by FIS, where jumping competitions are held on any of the half-dozen or so 120-metre hills. Distance alone is the criterion with these.

The more common 70- and 90-metre jumps are designated according to the lengths that can safely be jumped rather than physical distance from top to bottom. Generally a 70-metre hill will have a smaller tower and less steep in-run (the slope which the competitor skis down prior to take-off). All hills are constructed in such a way that adjustments may be made for varying weather conditions so that jumpers can safely reach distances of either 70 metres or 90 metres before the slope flattens out dangerously in the landing area.

Every hill has three important marks on the landing area. The judges determine the point where the average jumper should land, which is called the P point. The

We have take-off: and the ski jumper does not simply fall, he momentarily manages to fly

second critical mark is the table point or TP, which is where distance earns points. Any jumper who reaches the TP gains 60 points, and more if he goes beyond it. Distance judges stand every metre along the landing area to determine to the nearest half-metre the exact landing point, which is measured between the ankles of the jumper. The third mark is actually called the critical point or K for very good reason. Should the better jumpers start landing beyond point K, perhaps due to gusting wind, the judges have the right to stop the competition, cancel all points scored and begin again – as happened at Lake Placid during the last Olympic Games. When starting again the competitors have to take off from a lower starting-gate, which reduces the speed that they can generate on the in-run and thereby the distance jumped. The jury must watch the practice jumps to determine the best starting-gate.

Each competitor has two jumps, with distance and style counting half and half. On style, each skier starts with 20 marks, but points are deducted by the five judges for flaws in technique. The judges with the highest and lowest scores are disregarded but the points from the other three are added to the distance marks. Both distance and style marks are flashed on the scoreboard after each jump.

Style marks are only given from take-off, which should be really explosive. In the air the jumper should have good forward lean with hands by the sides, skis should be parallel and together, all movement in the air should be controlled, leading to a 'soft' landing with knees slightly flexed, preferably in the 'Telemark' position with one leg slightly in front of the other.

Ski Jumping 125

THE SKI JUMP

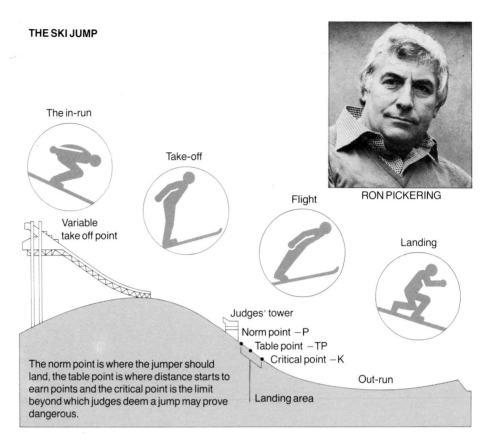

The in-run

Take-off

Flight

RON PICKERING

Variable take off point

Landing

Judges' tower

Norm point −P

Table point −TP

Critical point −K

The norm point is where the jumper should land, the table point is where distance starts to earn points and the critical point is the limit beyond which judges deem a jump may prove dangerous.

Out-run

Landing area

In the Winter Olympic Games there are separate competitions on both the 70- and 90-metre hills, and there is also a Nordic combined event involving both cross-country skiing over 15 kilometres and a 70-metre jumping competition. Outside the Olympics the major jumping event is the 'Springertournee' or 4 Hills competition, held in West Germany and Austria (at Oberstdorf, Garmisch, Innsbruck and Bischofshofen) each New Year. There is another great gathering in Oslo each year at the Holmonkollen, where it all began, which attracts up to 100,000 spectators. There are also World Championships and a recently introduced World Cup, as in skiing, which produces the best overall competitor of the year. For the Nordic World Championships in Oslo from 15 to 28 February, the Holmonkollen hill has been raised to accommodate jumps of around 85 metres.

Sondre Norheim, a Norwegian, is regarded as the father of ski jumping for it was he who in the middle of the nineteenth century devised the first effective ski binding which gave some control over his skis in flight. The first official competition in Oslo in 1879 produced a winning leap of twenty metres – it's a sobering thought that young schoolboys now achieve that using barn roofs as their in-run! Norway dominated the event until the mid-1950s, capturing fifteen out of eighteen possible jumping medals from the first six Winter Olympic

Games. Their all-time hero is Birger Ruud, one of three brilliant skiing brothers, who achieved a unique double by winning both a Nordic and an Alpine event in the 1936 Games. Not only did he successfully defend the jumping gold that he had won four years earlier, but also finished first in the downhill skiing event. Sixteen years after his first gold medal he earned another jumping silver in the 1948 Games.

During the 1950s and 60s other nations began to emerge, first Finland, Czechoslovakia, Austria, USSR, and then Japan in 1972 with a glorious 1–2–3 in the 70-metre jump led by Yukio Kasaya. Sapporo produced another surprise when Wojciech Fortuna captured Poland's first-ever ski medal in winning the 90-metre jump. When Austria staged the Games in 1976 the local heroes, Karl Schnabl and Tony Innauer, won gold and silver on the 70-metre hill. Schnabl also took the bronze on the 90-metre hill, which was won by East Germany's Hans-Georg Aschenbach. Tony Innauer secured a place for himself in the history books in 1980 at Lake Placid when he won the 70-metre jump. Jouko Tormanen of Finland won the 90-metre jump, beating Austria's Hubert Neuper, who in January won the 4 Hills tournament for the second year running.

The past season has been one of magnificent competition, with the balance of power swaying between Austria, Finland, East Germany and fast-improving Canada. Travelling to the various competitions, getting to know the competitors a little better each time, my respect for them grows at every encounter. These are not the dare-devils with the film star image and glamour of the downhillers. The commercial pressures and opportunities are certainly less, and each has his loyal band of supporters. In a crowd they could easily be sprinters, long jumpers or gymnasts – lean, muscular and rarely over six feet. Theirs is a quiet air of confidence, and their mutual respect creates instant cameraderie even among rival nations.

They certainly do not see their event as highly dangerous. I once sat through a film show with most of the world's best jumpers, where a whole series of disastrous jumps were shown. As the slow-motion camera focused on the whites of the eyes of the poor jumper who had reached the point of no return and suddenly realised it, I had to hold my breath. They simply collapsed with laughter at fools making elementary mistakes. They are quick to tell you that there are more fatal accidents on the downhill runs, but remember, sadly, the American Jeff Wright dying before helmets became obligatory in 1975.

Jumpers all begin as skiers who love the thrill of leaping over moguls and outcrops rather than skiing round them. To be born on skis is an advantage for, as Art Devlin, an American jumper and coach, once said, 'after eight it is too late – they must have the feel for jumping before they are old enough to understand it'.

So where does it all begin? The Americans have Steamboat Springs, the Canadians Thunder Bay, with a host of jumping areas from 20 metres to 90 metres. Norway and Finland have more than 500 at varying heights, and the Soviet Union have over 5000 registered jumpers with 164 paid coaches. Like the

Above: Coming in to land: Austria's Hubert Neuper, 4 Hills Tournament winner in 1980 and 1981. *Below:* Style marks also count in ski jumping: Armin Kogler, Austria's 1981 World Cup winner, takes off perfectly

East Germans, they have a synthetic jumping championships. There are now 326 jumping hills in the German Democratic Republic although they have no Alpine terrain and unreliable snow. Since 1954 they have used plastic ski slopes exclusively. These are like the ones we use for Alpine ski-training but with plastic landing areas. What is more, they are not far off producing the first 100-metre jump at their 'synthetic' championships.

Austria, on the other hand, has Stams, a university for skiers and ski jumpers just west of Innsbruck which not only demands high academic standards but, under the guidance of Professor Baldur Preiml, himself an Olympic bronze medallist, has created the most significant centre of excellence for ski jumping in the world. The sciences of aerodynamics and biomechanics are supported by a tremendous regime of physical efficiency. One thousand pre-season jumps are demanded in training, and in so doing each jumper climbs the equivalent of Mount Everest every winter. Stams also has a variety of plastic hills and it is not, therefore, surprising that it has produced for Austria the world's team champions and a long stream of individual champions with performances and personalities to match. Karl Schnabl and Tony Innauer have already been seen in 'The Superstars', and rightly so on past performances. Stealing the headlines now are Hubert ('Hupo') Neuper and Armin Kogler.

Hubert Neuper was the overall winner of the 4 Hills Tournament in 1980 and 1981 as well as Olympic silver medallist. Just twenty-one, this popular young man who looks rather like Donnie Osmond drives an Alfa Romeo and takes his family with him on competitions so that his mother can cook for him. He has just about the biggest following on the circuit. When only fourteen he asked to jump on a 90-metre hill for the first time and did 98.5 metres.

To be king of the 4 Hills is just about as high as you can get in ski jumping, but consider the claims of 22-year-old Armin Kogler, also from Stams, who, despite a disappointing Olympic Games, was runner-up to Neuper on the 4 Hills tournament. He broke the ski-flying world record in March with a leap of 180 metres, and went on to finish the season as overall World Cup champion.

In Lake Placid the first 'fore jumper' on the 90-metre hill was a 13-year-old local boy, Matt Terwilliger. He was too young to compete in the Games but jumped 90 metres or more to show the competitors the way. The youngest competitor in the Games was a 15-year-old half-Indian, half-Italian Canadian called Steve Collins (or 'Snowflake'), who leapt 114.5 metres. What's more his team-mate Horst Bulau, still only nineteen, was third overall in this year's World Cup – just behind Jari Puikkonen of Finland but ahead of Hubert Neuper. The most dramatic of all the winter sports events appears to be in good hands for a long while to come.

Oh yes, I almost forgot to mention that the British record for ski jumping is 61 metres, set by Guy Nixon at Davos in February 1931; and there is a world record for women – 98 metres by Anita Wold of Norway, set in Sapporo in January 1975.

16

NORDIC SKIING

John Samuel

Ask an experienced skier what is the biggest change he has seen in his favourite Alpine village in the last ten years, and his answer may be nothing to do with Alpine skiing. Not the by-pass, nor the discothèque either. It will be, in many villages, Nordic men (or women). You see them in most ski resorts these days, people of many nationalities in loose, thin waterproof tops known as cagouls rather than anoraks which are thicker and padded.

Many cross-country skiers wear breeches and stockings, and they ski on narrow, lightweight skis, with more pronounced curves at the tips, pushing forward on the balls of their feet, heels lifting with each stride, their lightweight shoes fixed only into toe bindings. As recreational skiers they are the joggers of the game, inheriting the rich tradition of cross-country skiing passed down by the Scandinavian countries, Norway, Sweden and Finland, where for centuries it was as much a means of getting around as snow shoes or the sled. Alpine skiing is only downhill. Cross-country is over undulating surfaces with as much uphill as down. In the hyped-up version at Olympic and World Championships (always in the same year but at a different venue from Alpine World Championships) the racer has as much relationship to the holidaymaker in Chamonix or Garmisch as Seb Coe has to the Hyde Park jogger.

The major men's events are 15 kilometres (9.3 miles), 30 (18.6) and 50 (31), a 40-kilometre relay, and the Nordic combined, which consists of a 70-metre jump on one day and a 15-kilometre cross-country the next. The women race 5, 10 and, this season, 20 kilometres, and a 20-kilometre relay. Jumping, whether on 70- or 90-metre hills, is also classified as Nordic skiing, and is part of a Nordic World Championship programme. This year Oslo hosts the Championships from 15 to 28 February, and will do so with the same sense of place and occasion as St Andrews staging the British Open Golf Championship. Until the 1970s the Nordic countries dominated their own sport, but the Russians and other East European countries have broken the monopoly, and America, Italy and Switzerland have all taken Olympic or World Championship medals in the 1970s,

reflecting the huge upswing in the activity in the snow countries.

Russia took six men's cross-country medals at Lake Placid in 1980 as she did in the Innsbruck Winter Olympics, Nikolai Zimyatov gaily telling US newsmen that his three golds made up for the Russian hockey defeat. XC, as it is known in the United States, televisually stays the orphan brother of ski jumping. Races are on prepared trails, participants in individual events taking off at 30-second intervals, with a passing racer given the right of way and the best time deciding. There are certain obvious overtaking situations towards the finish which can create excitement, but it is a hard format for the cameras, and the relays have the best head-to-head challenges.

After years of agonising and experiment, this season sees the innovation of World Cup programmes in all three of Jumping, Cross-country and Biathlon, a combination of cross-country and shooting. The Russians and East Germans are unhappy about commercial sponsorships, but as Bengt-Herman Nilsson, chairman of the FIS World Cup cross-country committee, has remarked, they are possibly a condition of survival. Cross-country will have nine events in even years (Olympics and World Championships take chunks out of the even-year seasons) and ten in odd years. The six best results of the nine or ten events will count, together with the two best of three events in Olympics and Worlds (unlike the Alpine World Cup, where they are kept strictly apart), plus a set of bonus points for the overall best in 15, 30 and 50 kilometres combined, in men's events, and 5, 10 and 20 kilometres in women's. Unlike Alpine, which scores 25 points for a first place down to one point for fifteenth, cross-country scores 26 for a first, 22 for a second, 19 for a third, and on a descending scale down to one point for twentieth place.

Biathlon has a separate World Championship at Minsk, Russia, from 15 to 21 February, and its own World Cup series with competitors counting their three best 20-kilometre and three best 10-kilometre results, each out of five events. First place gains 25 points and so on down to twenty-fifth place for a single point. One of the World Championship events should, if possible, be one of the World Cup events, but Winter Games events are not included.

Biathlon derives from the old military patrol race, and most competitors have an army background. Britain's team traditionally is recruited from army sources. Training is rigorous and long, demanding the conditioning of a marathoner with the skill and eye of an expert marksman. It is a major athletic accomplishment to pump along undulating trails for 20 kilometres ($12\frac{1}{2}$ miles) and at four points unsling a rifle and fire five rounds at alternately prone and standing paper targets 150 metres (or the length of a soccer pitch) distant. The prone target has an inner about the size of a man's hand (five inches in diameter), and the standing target is fourteen inches. A hit bears no penalty, an outer costs one minute and a miss two minutes. Forty minutes can be loaded on to a run of about seventy-five minutes if every target is missed.

Like XC itself, Biathlon suffers from the fact that it has a difficult TV format.

Biathletes take off: training is rigorous and long, demanding the conditioning of the marathoner and the eye of a marksman

At Olympic Games the relay tends to be more popular, with four-man teams making a mass start, each skiing $7\frac{1}{2}$ kilometres ($4\frac{1}{2}$ miles), stopping twice to shoot up to eight rounds at breakable targets. For each unbroken target a biathlete must ski a 20-metre penalty loop taking half a minute or more. This, though, has the excitement of the chase and one man perhaps obviously seen to be gaining on another.

The World Cup jumping programme lists thirteen competitions in the first stage until the World Championships in Oslo, with the best seven results to count. The second period, up until the finals on 27–28 March on the Planica 70-metre jump in Yugoslavia, has ten competitions with the best five to count. The World Championship's 70- and 90-metre events will also be included. The winner is the jumper with the best overall total.

GLOSSARY

Key: G= German; F= French; N= Norwegian.

Abfahrt (G): Downhill ski run (F: Descente), a test of speed, stamina and courage over two or three miles for men, and one to one and a half miles for women.

Alm (G): Mountain pasture, frequently used for ski trails in German-speaking countries.

Alpine skiing: Downhill, giant slalom and special slalom competitions.

Avalement (F): Racer or advanced technique at the beginning and end of fast turns involving quick, flexible bending of the knees with the feet thrust forward.

Base: Running surface of a ski, usually with a groove down the centre to assist with straight tracking. Composed of various plastic compounds to suit individual snow conditions and needs. In competition treated additionally with wax.

Biathlon: A combined cross-country skiing and shooting event, over 20 kilometres for individuals and 30 kilometres as a four-man relay. Controlled, not by FIS, but by the International Modern Pentathlon and Biathlon Union.

Bloodwagon: Sled for injured.

Bindings: Adjustable clips for holding boots to skis and releasing them in the event of a fall.

Calisthenics: Body-building exercises extensively undertaken by competitive racers.

Camber: Arch to the base of a ski.

Carved turn: A turn with the outside ski weighted on its inside edge. A pure, carved turn leaves a fine, thin line in the snow from the inside edge.

Christie: Family of turns. In a stem christie the outside ski fans out in a skidding style then returns to the parallel in traverse. In a parallel christie the skis are roughly side by side throughout the turn.

Circuit training: A set of exercises in sequence and without rest.

Citadin: races for competitors from non-skiing areas.

Combined event: Where a racer's results in two disciplines (eg downhill and special slalom) are aggregated to determine an overall position.

Compression: Flat or rising section usually following a steep pitch in a downhill run.

Control gates: Twin, beflagged poles through which skiers must turn or be disqualified.

Counter rotation: Angling of upper body so that the chest points down a slope when the legs are pointing across it.

Drag lifts: Means by which skiers are pulled up a slope; including 'T' bars for two people and button, disc or 'Poma' plates placed between the thighs for individuals.

Edging: Weighting the metal inside edges of skis to achieve turn.

Europa Cup: FIS circuit one level below World Cup.

Fall-line: Direct gravitational line below a skier.

FIS: Fédération Internationale de Ski, world governing body of skiing to which all national associations are affiliated. Headquarters in Berne, Switzerland.

Flats: Less steep slopes of a downhill course.

Flex: Bending property of a ski.

Föhn (G): Warm wind from the south.

Forerunner: Skier who runs the course before a race to test timing equipment and communications, and to help set a track for the first racers. Also Vorläufer (G).

Funicular: Tracked railway.

Giant Slalom – GS: Alpine race of about three quarters of a mile with open, rhythmic turns.

Gliding: Downhill technique keeping skis as flat as possible on the snow.

Gondola: Cabin cableway for two, four or more passengers, also known as a 'Bubble'.

Herringbone: Method of climbing, feet splayed, on skis.

Homologation: Tested, certified FIS courses.

Inside edge: Inside ski edge making the arc of a turn.

Inspection: Pre-race climb or sideslip down the side of a slalom course enabling racers to memorise gates.

In-run: Slope down which jumping competitors ski before take-off.

K-point: Critical point of a jumping hill beyond which skiers must not jump or judges will stop competition and restart with a shorter in-run. P-point represents the average distance a skier should jump, as determined by judges, and T-point the middle point where the competitor may achieve up to 60 points.

Loipe: Marked trail for Nordic skiers.

Nations Cup: National team competition in association with the Alpine World Cup.

Nordic skiing: Cross-country skiing and jumping, controlled by FIS. Cross-country is also known as Langlauf (G), Langrenn (N) and Ski de Fond (F).

Nordic Combined: A 15-kilometre cross-country run and 70-metre jumping competition scored on a combined points basis.

Parablack: Plastic boxes fitted towards the tip of skis to help prevent them crossing in downhill racing or soft snow.

Piste: Marked trail.

Pitch: Steep downhill section.

Plough turn: Most primitive form of ski turn with skis in a V, or plough, shape.

Pole: Ski stick (Stock (G), Baton (F)).

Pole plant: Use of the inside ski pole to initiate a turn, both timing it and helping with the unweighting.

Powder: New, low-temperature snow.

Pre-jump: Knee lift just before a knoll or ledge preventing a downhiller being thrown too far.

Schuss: Straight run.

Seeding: Placing of racers according to individual handicaps. The best handicapped get earlier start numbers and better snow. Handicaps are based on a points system, updated three times a season according to a racer's best two results in each discipline. The lower the points the better. Points are assessed according to the quality of the field. Minimum qualifications for World Cup events in 1981–2 are: Men – Dh & Sl 37; GS 34. Women – 74 in each discipline.

Sidecut: Line of ski from tip to tail with waisted effect.

Sideslip: Flattening of skis against a slope for controlled slipping downwards or diagonally.

Ski Flying: Jumping from hills in excess of 90 metres (usually 120 metres) with distance alone the criterion.

Ski Jumping: Jumping from hills, usually of 70 or 90 metres, scored on distance and style. The hills are designated according to lengths that can safely be jumped and not physical distance from top to bottom.

Ski stoppers: U-shaped spring-clips with prongs attached to many bindings, which dig into the snow and stop a ski from running away dangerously after a fall.

Skid: Turn where edge fails to bite instantly, costing precious time.

Special Slalom: Short race decided on the aggregate time of two runs testing speed and turning techniques. Parallel slalom involves two racers on adjacent courses, the fastest over the two runs going into the next round, and so on until the final.

Stem: Outward fanning movement of ski to start a turn (*see* Christie).

Super Giant Slalom: Longer, $1\frac{1}{4}$-mile giant slalom of about 2-minute duration with which FIS are experimenting in 1982–3. Terrain will be more varied than a conventional GS with two jumps of 10–20 metres, and results decided on one run rather than two.

Swing: Shallow turn.

Traverse: Diagonal movement over a slope.

Tuck: Crouched position of a downhill racer.

Unweighting: Slight upward movement of the body, momentarily easing pressure on skis for the initiation of a turn. Downweighting can secure the same effect.

Wedel: Short, fast-linked turns on flat or near-flat skis down the fall-line.

White Circus: World Cup circuit.

White-out: Sudden flat light where it becomes difficult to distinguish irregularities in the snow.

World Championships: Held every four years in their own right at different venues, and combined with Olympic Games to make a two-year award of medals.

World Cup: Season-long competitions in Alpine, cross-country and jumping. Points are aggregated from individual events to provide overall champions. Alpine events also have individual winners in Downhill, Giant Slalom and Special Slalom.

LEADING WORLD SKIERS

In the following biographical information on world skiers seeded in the top fifteen of each discipline at the start of the 1981-2 season the skier's name is followed by his nationality, date of birth and home town. World Cup overall positions are then listed, followed by medal-winning performances in World Championships and Olympic Games. Finally 1980–1 World Cup results in the top ten are given (preceded by the date 1981).

The following abbreviations are used: WC – World Championships; OG – Olympic Games; Dh – Downhill; Sl – Slalom; GS – Giant Slalom. In the overall results the last two figures of the year only are used. Nationalities for biographies and records are indicated by the normal FIS system:

AUT Austria
BEL Belgium
BRD West Germany
BUL Bulgaria
CAN Canada
FRA France
IRE Ireland

ITA Italy
JPN Japan
JUG Yugoslavia
LIE Liechtenstein
LUX Luxembourg
NOR Norway
POL Poland

SOV USSR
SPA Spain
SUI Switzerland
SWE Sweden
TCH Czechoslovakia
USA United States

MEN

Vladimir Andreev

Paolo de Chiesa

Andreev, Vladimir, SOV
9.2.58, Noskh.
Overall: 1979 – 91; 80 – 51; 81 –
20. **1981** Sl: 2nd Kitzbuehel; 4th St
Anton; 3rd Oslo; 6th Are.

Buergler, Toni, SUI
17.8.57, Rickenbach.
Overall: 1979 – 20; 80 – 49; 81 –
24. **1981** Dh: 9th Cortina; 5th Garmisch; 1st Wengen; 4th Aspen 2.

de Chiesa, Paolo, ITA
14.3.56, Saluzzo.
Overall: 1975 – 10; 76 – 40; 77 –
49; 78 – 23; 80 – 45; 81 – 36. **1981**
Sl: 10th Oberstaufen; 5th Wengen;
7th St Anton; 9th Furano.

Enn, Hans, AUT
10.5.58, Hinteglemm.
Overall: 1976 – 55; 77 – 35; 78 –
38; 79 – 12; 80 – 7; 81 – 14. OG 80:
GS 3rd. **1981** Sl: 8th Oberstaufen.
GS: 4th Madonna di Campiglio; 2nd
Ebnat-Kappel; 2nd Schladming.

Fjaellberg, Bengt, SWE
15.9.61, Tarnaby.
Overall: 1981 – 33. **1981** Sl: 2nd
Oslo; 4th Are; 6th Borovetz.

Toni Buergler

Hans Enn

Bengt Fjaellberg

Paul Frommelt

Marc Girardelli

Piero Gros

Fournier, Jean-Luc, SUI
23.9.56, Nendaz.
Overall: 1977 – 58; 78 – 19; 79 –
30; 80 – 53; 81 – 21. **1981** GS: 3rd
Ebnat-Kappel; 7th Adelboden; 3rd
Schladming; 4th Are; 5th Aspen; 10th
Laax.

Frommelt, Paul, LIE
9.8.57, Schaan.
Overall: 1976 – 55; 77 – 10; 78 –
33; 79 – 17; 80 – 26; 81 – 17. WC 78:
Sl 3rd. **1981** Sl: 2nd Madonna di
Campiglio; 3rd Garmisch; 1st Ober-
staufen; 9th Wengen; 7th Oslo; 8th
Are.

Gaspoz, Joel, SUI
25.9.62, Morgins.
Overall: 1980 – 17; 81 – 11. **1981**
Sl: 8th Madonna di Campiglio; 5th
Kitzbuehel. GS: 9th Ebnat-Kappel;
2nd Morzine; 4th Voss; 4th Aspen;
4th Furano; 3rd Borovetz.

Girardelli, Marc, LUX
6.10.60, Lustenau (Austria).
Overall: 1980 – 84; 81 – 26. **1981**
Sl: 2nd Wengen; 8th Borovetz. GS:
7th Aspen.

Grissmann, Werner, AUT
21.1.52, Lienz.
Overall: 1973 – 25; 74 – 16; 75 – 8;
76 – 22; 77 – 20; 78 – 22; 79 – 33;
80 – 21; 81 – 46. WC 78: Dh 3rd.
1981 Dh: 10th Kitzbuehel; 8th Aspen
1; 8th Aspen 2.

Gros, Piero, ITA
30.10.54, Sauze d'Ouix.
Overall: 1973 – 10; 74 – 1; 75 – 4;
76 – 2; 77 – 4; 78 – 9; 79 – 4; 80 –
29; 81 – 28. WC 78: Sl 2nd. **1981** Sl:
7th Madonna di Campiglio; 5th Garmisch; 7th Oberstaufen; 8th Oslo; 5th
Are.

Gruber, Franz, AUT
8.11.59, Molln.
Overall: 1979 – 32; 80 – 45; 81 –
25. **1981** Sl: 9th Madonna di Campiglio; 9th Oberstaufen; 3rd Are; 7th
Furano; 9th Borovetz. GS: 10th Ebnat-
Kappel.

Halsnes, Jarle, NOR
4.5.57, Sauda.
Overall: 1980 – 24; 81 – 13. **1981**
Sl: 10th Wengen; 3rd St Anton; 9th
Oslo; 10th Are; 8th Furano; 7th Boro-

Jean-Luc Fournier

Joel Gaspoz

Werner Grissmann

Franz Gruber

Jarle Halsnes

Bojan Krizaj

Krizaj, Bojan, JUG
3.1.57, Kranj.
Overall: 1977 – 43; 78 – 20; 79 – 8;
80 – 4; 81 – 6. **1981** Sl: 3rd Madonna di Campiglio; 4th Garmisch; 1st Wengen; 8th St Anton; 2nd Furano; 10th Borovetz. GS: 10th Madonna di Campiglio; 3rd Morzine; 10th Are; 7th Borovetz.

Luescher, Peter, SUI
14.10.56, Romanshorn.
Overall: 1975 – 52; 76 – 25; 77 – 36; 78 – 16; 79 – 1; 80 – 10; 81 – 58.
1981 Dh: 9th Val Gardena.

Luethy, Jacques, SUI
11.7.59, Charmey.
Overall: 1979 – 13; 80 – 6; 81 – 15.
OG 80: Sl 3rd. **1981** GS: 7th Madonna di Campiglio; 6th Ebnat-Kappel; 9th Morzine; 4th Adelboden; 5th Schladming; 10th Voss; 5th Are; 8th Furano.

Helmut Hoeflehner

Peter Luescher

vetz. GS: 5th Adelboden; 9th Schladming; 5th Voss; 8th Are; 4th Borovetz; 8th Laax.

Hoeflehner, Helmut, AUT
24.11.59, Gumpenberg.
Overall: 1980 – 53; 81 – 30. **1981** Dh: 10th Val Gardena; 4th Garmisch; 6th Kitzbuehel; 9th Wengen; 6th Aspen 1.

Irwin, Dave, CAN
12.7.54, Loch Lemond.
Overall: 1975 – 45; 76 – 17; 79 – 71; 80 – 53; 81 – 52. **1981** Dh: 5th Val d'Isère.

Jaeger, Gerhard, AUT
8.2.58, Filzmoos.
GS: 3rd Madonna di Campiglio; 2nd Furano.

Klammer, Franz, AUT
3.12.53, Mooswald.
Overall: 1973 – 8; 74 – 5; 75 – 3; 76 – 4; 77 – 3; 78 – 5; 79 – 51; 80 – 33; 81 – 40. WC 74: Dh 2nd. OG 76:
Overall: 1978 – 51; 81 – 35. **1981** Dh 1st. **1981** Dh: 10th Val Gardena; 6th Cortina; 8th St Moritz; 7th Wengen.

Dave Irwin

Jacques Luethy

Gerhard Jaeger

Franz Klammer

Mahre, Phil, USA
10.5.57, White Pass, Wash.
Overall: 1976 – 14; 77 – 9; 78 – 2;
79 – 3; 80 – 3; 81 – 1. OG 80: Sl 2nd.
1981 Dh: 9th Kitzbuehel. Sl: 10th
Garmisch; 4th Oberstaufen; 2nd St
Anton; 4th Oslo; 1st Are; 1st Furano;
3rd Borovetz. GS: 8th Madonna di
Campiglio; 4th Ebnat-Kappel; 4th
Morzine; 8th Adelboden; 6th Schladming; 6th Voss; 3rd Are; 1st Aspen;
5th Borovetz, 2nd Laax.

Mahre, Steve, USA
10.5.57, White Pass, Wash.

Phil Mahre

Steve Mahre

Overall: 1976 – 27; 77 – 43; 78 –
23; 79 – 10; 80 – 12; 81 – 4. **1981**
Sl: 1st Garmisch; 3rd Oberstaufen; 7th
Wengen; 6th Oslo; 6th Furano; 2nd
Borovetz. GS: 5th Madonna di Cam-
piglio; 3rd Aspen; 6th Borovetz.

Makeev, Vladimir, SOV
10.9.57, Kemehovo.
Overall: 1979 – 41; 81 – 48. **1981**
Dh: 9th Val d'Isère; 4th Wengen; 9th
St Anton.

Mally, Peter, ITA
9.10.58, Merano.
Overall: 1978 – 46; 79 – 45; 80 –
75; 81 – 59. **1981** Sl: 4th Madonna
di Campiglio.

Vladimir Makeev

Peter Mally

Mueller, Peter, SUI
6.10.57, Adliswil.
Overall: 1977 – 24; 78 – 36; 79 –
15; 80 – 9; 81 – 5. **1981** Dh: 1st Val
Gardena; 3rd Cortina; 3rd St Moritz;
2nd Garmisch; 2nd Kitzbuehel; 4th
Aspen 1; 5th Aspen 2.

Noeckler, Bruno, ITA
6.10.56, Predoi.
Overall: 1976 – 35; 77 – 22; 78 –
42; 79 – 96; 80 – 27; 81 – 16. **1981**
Sl: 8th Garmisch. GS: 6th Madonna
di Campiglio; 8th Ebnat-Kappel; 5th
Morzine; 10th Adelboden; 4th Schladming; 3rd Voss; 8th Aspen; 10th Furano.

Peter Mueller

Bruno Noeckler

Orlainsky, Christian, AUT
17.2.62, Tschagguns.
Overall: 1979 – 26; 80 – 18; 81 –
10. **1981** Sl: 5th Oberstaufen; 3rd
Kitzbuehel; 6th Wengen. GS: 1st Ebnat-Kappel; 10th Morzine; 2nd Adelboden; 8th Schladming.

Christian Orlainsky

Steve Podborski

Wolfram Ortner

Ken Read

Gerhard Pfaffenbichler

Odd Soerli

Ortner, Wolfram, AUT
10.3.60, Bad Kleinkirchheim.
Overall: 1978 – 46; 79 – 35; 81 –
39. **1981** Sl: 5th St Anton. GS: 8th
Voss; 7th Are.

Pfaffenbichler, Gerhard, AUT
26.3.61, Unken.
Overall: 1981 – 28. **1981** Dh: 8th
Val d'Isère; 4th St Anton; 3rd Aspen
1; 6th Aspen 2.

Podborski, Steve, CAN
25.7.57, Don Mills.
Overall: 1976 – 43; 78 – 31; 79 –
36; 80 – 30; 81 – 9. OG 80: Dh 3rd.
1981 Dh: 3rd Val d'Isère; 3rd Val Gardena; 10th Cortina; 1st St Moritz; 1st
Garmisch; 1st Kitzbuehel; 3rd Wengen; 3rd St Anton; 10th Aspen 1; 2nd
Aspen 2.

Popangelov, Peter, BUL
31.1.59, Samokov.
Overall: 1977 – 58; 78 – 13; 79 –
19; 80 – 13; 81 – 50. **1981** Sl: 2nd
Garmisch.

Read, Ken, CAN
6.11.55, Calgary.
Overall: 1975 – 49; 76 – 24; 77 –
58; 78 – 11; 79 – 22; 80 – 11; 81 –
38. **1981** Dh: 2nd Val d'Isère; 6th
Cortina; 9th St Moritz.

Resch, Erwin, AUT
4.3.61, Mariapfarr.
Overall: 1979 – 63; 81 – 42. **1981**
Dh: 4th Val Gardena; 9th Garmisch;
7th Aspen.

Soerli, Odd, NOR
29.11.54, Oslo.
Overall: 1980 – 41; 81 – 46. **1981**
Sl: 6th St Anton. GS: 6th Are.

Spiess, Uli, AUT
15.8.55, Mayrhofen.
Overall: 1977 – 37; 78 – 12; 79 –
27; 80 – 36; 81 – 23. **1981** Dh: 1st
Val d'Isère; 5th Val Gardena; 2nd Cortina.

Stenmark, Ingemar, SWE
18.3.56, Tarnaby.
Overall: 1974 – 12; 75 – 2; 76 – 1;
77 – 1; 78 – 1; 79 – 5; 80 – 2; 81 – 2.
WC 78: Sl 1st; GS 1st. OG 76: GS
3rd. OG 80: Sl 1st; GS 1st. **1981** Sl:
1st Madonna di Campiglio; 2nd Oberstaufen; 1st Kitzbuehel; 3rd Wengen;
1st St Anton; 1st Oslo; 2nd Are; 3rd
Furano; 5th Borovetz. GS: 1st Madonna di Campiglio; 1st Morzine; 1st
Adelboden; 1st Schladming; 1st Voss;
1st Are; 2nd Aspen; 3rd Furano; 2nd
Borovetz; 3rd Laax.

Uli Spiess

Peter Popangelov

Ingemar Stenmark

Leonhard Stock

Boris Strel

Valeri Tsyganov

Josef Walcher

Harti Weirather

Andreas Wenzel

Peter Wirnsberger

Alexander Zhirov

Stock, Leonhard, AUT
14.3.58, Zell am Ziller.
Overall: 1977 – 31; 78 – 21; 79 – 2;
80 – 45; 81 – 12. OG 80: Dh 1st.
1981 Dh: 6th Val Gardena; 5th Cortina; 5th St Moritz; 10th Aspen 2. GS: 8th Morzine; 5th Furano; 6th Laax.

Strel, Boris, JUG
20.10.59, Skofja Loka.
Overall: 1979 – 25; 80 – 25; 81 – 21. **1981** GS: 3rd Adelboden; 10th Schladming; 9th Furano; 9th Borovetz.

Tsyganov, Valeri, SOV
4.2.61, Moscow.
Overall: 1979 – 68; 80 – 28; 81 – 18. **1981** Dh: 5th Wengen; 1st Aspen 1.

Walcher, Josef, AUT
8.12.54, Schladming.
Overall: 1973 – 28; 74 – 29; 75 – 23; 76 – 30; 77 – 8; 78 – 7; 79 – 39; 80 – 22; 81 – 41. WC 78: Dh 1st.
1981 Dh: 7th St Moritz; 8th Wengen; 5th St Anton.

Weirather, Harti, AUT
25.1.58, Reutte.
Overall: 1979 – 53; 80 – 15; 81 – 8.
1981 Dh: 2nd Val Gardena; 1st Cortina; 6th Wengen; 1st St Anton; 2nd Aspen 1; 1st Aspen 2.

Wenzel, Andreas, LIE
18.3.58, Planken.
Overall: 1977 – 21; 78 – 3; 79 – 6; 80 – 1; 81 – 7. WC 78: GS 2nd; Comb. 1st. OG 76: Sl 1st. OG 80: GS 2nd.
1981 Sl: 5th Furano; 4th Borovetz. GS: 9th Madonna di Campiglio; 7th Ebnat-Kappel; 6th Morzine; 9th Adelboden.

Wirnsberger, Peter, AUT
13.9.58, Vordernberg.
Overall: 1977 – 24; 78 – 17; 79 – 16; 80 – 19; 81 – 18. OG 80: Dh 2nd.
1981 Dh: 2nd St Moritz; 7th Garmisch; 3rd Kitzbuehel; 10th Wengen; 2nd St Anton; 7th Aspen 1.

Zhirov, Alexander, SOV
1959.
Overall: 1980 – 14; 81 – 3. **1981** Sl: 6th Oberstaufen; 9th Kitzbuehel; 4th Wengen; 5th Oslo; 4th Furano; 1st Borovetz. GS: 2nd Madonna di Campiglio; 7th Schladming; 2nd Voss; 2nd Are; 6th Aspen; 1st Furano; 1st Borovetz; 1st Laax.

Bieler, Wanda, ITA
7.7.59, Gressoney St Jean.
Overall: 1976 – 32; 78 – 30; 79 – 56; 80 – 26; 81 – 17. **1981** Sl: 7th Zwiesel. GS: 4th Limone Piemonte; 6th Haute-Nendaz; 5th Les Gets; 4th Zwiesel; 3rd Aspen.

Charvatova, Olga, TCH
11.6.62, Gottwaldov.
Overall: 1979 – 17; 80 – 34; 81 – 15. **1981** Dh: 9th Altenmarkt. Sl: 9th Schruns; 10th Crans-Montana; 4th Zwiesel. GS: 9th Val d'Isère; 8th Furano; 6th Wangs.

Cooper, Christine, USA
8.10.59, Sun Valley, Id.
Overall: 1977 – 35; 78 – 18; 79 – 23; 80 – 18; 81 – 4. **1981** Sl: 5th Piancavallo; 7th Altenmarkt; 6th Bormio; 6th Schruns; 2nd Crans-Montana; 2nd Les Diablerets; 3rd Zwiesel; 2nd Furano. GS: 8th Limone Piemonte; 4th Haute-Nendaz; 5th Zwiesel; 5th Maribor; 3rd Furano; 2nd Wangs.

de Agostini, Doris, SUI
28.4.58, Airolo.
Overall: 1976 – 24; 77 – 28; 79 – 42; 80 – 21; 81 – 13. WC 78: Dh 3rd. **1981** Dh: 3rd Piancavallo; 2nd Altenmarkt; 2nd Pfronten; 1st Schruns; 2nd Crans-Montana; 1st Megève 1; 2nd Megève 2; 4th Haus; 6th Aspen.

Eberle, Ingrid, AUT
3.6.57, Dornbirn.
Overall: 1974 – 34; 76 – 43; 77 – 24; 78 – 16; 80 – 16; 81 – 41. **1981** Dh: 7th Altenmarkt.

Epple, Irene, BRD
18.6.57, Seeg-Allgau.
Overall: 1973 – 41; 74 – 34; 75 – 13; 76 – 10; 77 – 18; 78 – 11; 79 – 3; 80 – 5; 81 – 5. WC 78: Dh 2nd. OG 80: GS 2nd. **1981** Dh: 3rd Val d'Isère; 5th Altenmarkt; 6th Pfronten; 3rd Schruns; 6th Megève 1; 2nd Haus. GS: 1st Val d'Isère; 3rd Haute-Nendaz; 3rd Maribor; 8th Aspen; 5th Furano; 4th Wangs.

Epple, Maria, BRD
11.3.59, Seeg-Allgau.
Overall: 1976 – 38; 77 – 33; 78 – 7; 80 – 29; 81 – 14. WC 78; GS 1st. **1981** Sl: 5th Zwiesel; 3rd Furano. GS: 4th Les Gets; 1st Zwiesel; 2nd Maribor; 9th Aspen; 10th Furano; 9th Wangs.

Ingrid Eberle

Wanda Bieler

Christine Cooper

Irene Epple

Olga Charvatova

Doris de Agostini

Maria Epple

Abigail Fisher

Claudia Giordani

Zoe Haas

Christa Kinshofer

Fisher, Abigail, USA
30.8.57, South Conway, NH.
Overall: 1975 – 32; 76 – 27; 77 – 17; 78 – 15; 79 – 27; 80 – 22; 81 – 29. **1981** Sl: 9th Piancavallo; 4th Crans-Montana.

Fjeldstad, Torill, NOR
22.5.58, Lillehammer.
Overall: 1980 – 36; 81 – 20. **1981** Dh: 2nd Piancavallo; 3rd Altenmarkt; 3rd Megève 1; 6th Haus.

Flanders, Holly Beth, USA
26.12.57, Manchester, NH.
Overall: 1979 – 29; 80 – 23; 81 – 19. **1981** Dh: 7th Piancavallo; 3rd Pfronten; 8th Crans-Montana; 4th Megève 1; 4th Megève 2; 8th Haus; 4th Aspen.

Giordani, Claudia, ITA
27.10.55, Milan.
Overall: 1973 – 22; 74 – 13; 75 – 18; 76 – 11; 77 – 8; 78 – 37; 79 – 10; 80 – 8; 81 – 21. OG 76: Sl 2nd. **1981** Sl: 8th Altenmarkt; 5th Bormio; 2nd Schruns. GS: 9th Limone Piemonte; 9th Les Gets.

Gros-Gaudenier, Marie-Cécile,
FRA 18.6.60, Scionzier.
Overall: 1979 – 43; 80 – 64; 81 – 37. **1981** Dh: 5th Crans-Montana; 10th Megève 1; 8th Megève 2.

Haas, Zoe, SUI
24.1.62, Engelberg.
Overall: 1979 – 49; 80 – 69; 81 – 24. **1981** Dh: 5th Val d'Isère; 9th Aspen. GS: 10th Limone Piemonte; 9th Maribor.

Haecher, Traudl, BRD
31.12.62, Schleching.
Overall: 1981 – 25. **1981** Dh: 8th Megève 1. GS: 6th Aspen; 7th Wangs.

Hess, Erika, SUI
6.3.62, Grafenort.
Overall: 1978 – 28; 79 – 15; 80 – 7; 81 – 2. OG 80: Sl 3rd. **1981** Sl: 2nd Piancavallo; 3rd Bormio; 1st Schruns; 1st Crans-Montana; 1st Les Diablerets; 1st Zwiesel; 1st Furano; 1st Wangs. GS: 10th Val d'Isère; 5th Limone Piemonte; 4th Maribor; 2nd Aspen; 6th Furano; 1st Wangs.

Elisabeth Kirchler

Holly Beth Flanders

Erika Hess

Cindy Nelson

Kinshofer, Christa, BRD
24.1.61, Miesbach.
Overall: 1977 – 40; 79 – 8; 80 – 11; 81 – 9. OG 80: Sl 2nd. **1981** Dh: 10th Val d'Isère; 3rd Crans-Montana. Sl: 2nd Altenmarkt. GS: 3rd Val d'Isère; 8th Haute-Nendaz; 2nd Les Gets; 2nd Zwiesel.

Kirchler, Elisabeth, AUT
17.11.63, Lanersbach.
Overall: 1981 – 33. **1981** Dh: 9th Haus; 1st Aspen.

Konzett, Ursula, LIE
15.11.59, Triesen.
Overall: 1977 – 28; 78 – 22; 79 – 40; 80 – 25; 81 – 38. **1981** Sl: 8th Piancavallo; 4th Bormio; 6th Crans-Montana.

Kreiner, Kathy, CAN
4.5.57, Timmins.
Overall: 1972 – 31; 73 – 24; 74 – 10; 75 – 12; 76 – 23; 77 – 13; 78 – 25; 79 – 39; 80 – 31; 81 – 27. OG 76: GS 1st. **1981** Dh: 2nd Val d'Isère; 7th Megève 1.

Macchi, Piera, ITA
5.3.59, Varese.
Overall: 1979 – 52; 80 – 38; 81 – 26. **1981** Sl: 4th Altenmarkt; 8th Schruns; 8th Crans-Montana; 4th Les Diablerets; 5th Furano.

McKinney, Tamara, USA
16.10.62, Olympic Valley, Ca.
Overall: 1979 – 25; 80 – 14; 81 – 6. **1981** Sl: 3rd Schruns; 7th Les Diablerets; 4th Furano; 5th Wangs. GS: 6th Val d'Isère; 1st Haute-Nendaz; 1st Les Gets; 3rd Zwiesel; 7th Maribor; 1st Aspen; 4th Furano.

Moesenlechner, Regine, BRD
1.4.61, Inzell.
Overall: 1975 – 39; 78 – 28; 79 – 12; 80 – 15; 81 – 21. **1981** Dh: 7th Haus; 2nd Aspen. Sl: 7th Schruns.

Nelson, Cindy, USA
19.8.56, Lutsen, Minn.
Overall: 1974 – 15; 75 – 8; 76 – 8; 77 – 19; 78 – 5; 79 – 4; 80 – 10; 81 – 8. OG 76: Dh 3rd. **1981** Dh: 5th Pfronten; 2nd Schruns; 9th Crans-Montana; 9th Megève 2; 3rd Aspen. Sl: 10th Altenmarkt; 8th Bormio; 9th Furano. GS: 10th Haute-Nendaz; 6th Maribor; 5th Aspen; 6th Furano; 5th Wangs.

Ursula Konzett

Kathy Kreiner

Tamara McKinney

Regine Moesenlechner

Nadezhda Patrakeeva

Patrakeeva, Nadezhda, SOV
11.4.59.
Overall: 1977 – 59; 80 – 20; 81 – 27. **1981** Sl: 4th Piancavallo; 9th Altenmarkt; 2nd Bormio; 10th Furano.

Pelen, Perrine, FRA
3.7.60, Grenoble.
Overall: 1977 – 7; 78 – 6; 79 – 9; 80 – 4; 81 – 6. OG 80: GS 3rd. **1981** Sl: 6th Piancavallo; 1st Altenmarkt; 1st Bormio; 5th Les Diablerets; 8th Zwiesel; 7th Furano; 6th Wangs.

Perrine Pelen

Edith Peter

Heidi Preuss

Maria Rosa Quario

Lea Soelkner

Gerry Sorensen

Peter, Edith, AUT
19.2.58, Alberschwende.
Overall: 1979 – 26; 81 – 35. **1981**
Dh: 9th Piancavallo; 4th Pfronten; 7th
Schruns; 10th Megève 2.

Preuss, Heidi, USA
18.3.61, Lakeport, NH.
Overall: 1979 – 18; 80 – 12; 81 –
30. **1981** Dh: 7th Altenmarkt; 5th
Schruns.

Proell, Cornelia, AUT
21.1.61, Kleinarl.
Overall: 1979 – 36; 80 – 27; 81 –
16. **1981** Dh: 7th Val d'Isère; 6th
Piancavallo; 4th Altenmarkt; 1st Pfronten; 5th Megève 1; 3rd Megève 2; 3rd
Haus.

Quario, Maria Rosa, ITA
24.5.61, Milan
Overall: 1979 – 13; 80 – 31; 81 –
18. **1981** Sl: 3rd Piancavallo; 6th
Altenmarkt; 10th Schruns. GS: 7th
Limone Piemonte; 8th Les Gets; 10th
Aspen.

Serrat, Fabienne, FRA
5.7.56, Bourg d'Oisan.
Overall: 1973 – 20; 74 – 5; 75 – 5;
76 – 7; 77 – 9; 78 – 4; 79 – 6; 80 – 6;
81 – 10. WC 74: GS 1st. **1981** Sl:
1st Piancavallo; 5th Altenmarkt; 6th
Bormio; 9th Crans-Montana; 6th Les
Diablerets; 9th Wangs. GS: 4th Val
d'Isère; 3rd Limone Piemonte; 9th
Zwiesel.

Soelkner, Lea, AUT
24.12.58, Tauplitz.
Overall: 1976 – 32; 77 – 15; 78 – 9;
79 – 11; 80 – 17; 81 – 31. WC 78: Sl
1st. **1981** Dh: 4th Val d'Isère; 6th
Altenmarkt.

Soltysova, Jana, TCH
30.9.59, Kezmarok.
Overall: 1976 – 40; 79 – 33; 80 –
13; 81 – 21. **1981** Dh: 10th Piancavallo; 1st Altenmarkt; 9th Pfronten;
4th Crans-Montana; 7th Megève 2.

Sorensen, Gerry, CAN
1959, Kimberley.
Overall: 1981 – 45. **1981** Dh: 5th
Megève 2; 1st Haus.

Cornelia Proell

Fabienne Serrat

Jana Soltysova

Maria Walliser

Hanni Wenzel

Wenzel, Hanni, LIE
14.12.56, Planken.
Overall: 1972 – 40; 73 – 5; 74 – 3;
75 – 2; 76 – 9; 77 – 5; 78 – 1; 79 – 2;
80 – 1; 81 – 3. WC 74: Sl 1st. OG 76:
Sl 3rd. OG 80: Dh 2nd; Sl 1st; GS
1st. **1981** Dh: 8th Pfronten; 6th
Schruns; 5th Haus; 8th Aspen. Sl: 4th
Schruns; 3rd Crans-Montana; 6th
Zwiesel; 6th Furano; 4th Wangs. GS:
2nd Haute-Nendaz; 3rd Les Gets; 8th
Zwiesel; 8th Maribor; 2nd Furano;
3rd Wangs.

Daniela Zini

Walliser, Maria, SUI
27.5.63, Mosnang.
Overall: 1981 – 12. **1981** Dh: 9th
Val d'Isère; 7th Crans-Montana; 8th
Megève 1; 5th Megève 2; 10th Haus.
Sl: 9th Zwiesel; 3rd Wangs.

Zini, Daniela, ITA
30.5.59, Livigno.
Overall: 1979 – 14; 80 – 9; 81 – 11.
1981 Sl: 3rd Altenmarkt; 5th Schruns;
5th Crans-Montana; 3rd Les Diablerets; 2nd Zwiesel; 8th Furano; 2nd
Wangs. GS: 8th Val d'Isère; 2nd
Limone Piemonte; 7th Haute-Nendaz;
6th Les Gets; 7th Aspen.

WORLD CUP RECORDS 1967-81

MEN'S OVERALL 1967–81

1967

1 J C Killy	FRA	225
2 H Messner	AUT	114
3 G Perillat	FRA	108
4 L Lacroix	FRA	93
5 G Mauduit	FRA	82
6 J Heuga	USA	70

1968

1 J C Killy	FRA	200
2 D. Giovanoli	SUI	119
3 H Huber	AUT	112
4 G Nenning	AUT	102
5 G Perillat	FRA	83
6 E Bruggmann	SUI	80

1969

1 K Schranz	AUT	182
2 J N Augert	FRA	123
3 R Tritscher	AUT	108
4 A Matt	AUT	104
5 A Penz	FRA	98
6 H Duvillard	FRA	91

1970

1 K Schranz	AUT	148
2 P Russel	FRA	145
3 G Thoeni	ITA	140
4 J N Augert	FRA	120
5 A Penz	FRA	119
6 D Giovanoli	SUI	116

1971

1 G Thoeni	ITA	155
2 H Duvillard	FRA	135
3 P Russel	FRA	125
4 J N Augert	FRA	107
5 B Russi	SUI	95
6 E Bruggmann	SUI	94

1972

1 G Thoeni	ITA	154
2 H Duvillard	FRA	142
3 E Bruggmann	SUI	140
4 J N Augert	FRA	125
5 B Russi	SUI	114
6 A Bachleda	POL	112

1973

1 G Thoeni	ITA	168
2 D Zwilling	AUT	151
3 R Collombin	SUI	131
4 C Neureuther	BRD	120
H Hinterseer	AUT	120
6 B Russi	SUI	106

1974

1 P Gros	ITA	181
2 G Thoeni	ITA	165
3 H Hinterseer	AUT	162
4 R Collombin	SUI	140
5 F Klammer	AUT	125
6 E Stricker	ITA	98

1975

1 G Thoeni	ITA	250
2 I Stenmark	SWE	245
3 F Klammer	AUT	240
4 P Gros	ITA	196
5 E Haker	NOR	147
6 H Hinterseer	AUT	117

1976

1	I Stenmark	SWE	249
2	P Gros	ITA	205
3	G Thoeni	ITA	190
4	F Klammer	AUT	181
5	H Hinterseer	AUT	98
	W Tresh	SUI	98

1977

1	I Stenmark	SWE	339
2	K Heidegger	AUT	250
3	F Klammer	AUT	203
4	P Gros	ITA	165
5	B Russi	SUI	148
6	G Thoeni	ITA	145

1978

1	I Stenmark	SWE	150
2	P Mahre	USA	116
3	A Wenzel	LIE	100
4	K Heidegger	AUT	95
5	F Klammer	AUT	70
	H Plank	ITA	70

1979

1	P Luescher	SUI	186
2	L Stock	AUT	163
3	P Mahre	USA	155
4	P Gros	ITA	152
5	I Stenmark	SWE	150
6	A Wenzel	LIE	148

1980

1	A Wenzel	LIE	204
2	I Stenmark	SWE	200
3	P Mahre	USA	132
4	B Krizaj	YUG	131
5	A Steiner	AUT	130
6	J Luethy	SUI	116
7	H Enn	AUT	100
8	H Plank	ITA	91
9	P Mueller	SUI	87
	P Luescher	SUI	87

1981

1	Phil Mahre	USA	266
2	Ingemar Stenmark	SWE	260

3	Alexander Zhirov	USA	185
4	Steve Mahre	USA	155
5	Peter Mueller	SUI	140
6	Bojan Krizaj	JUG	137
7	Andreas Wenzel	LIE	130
8	Harti Weirather	AUT	115
9	Steve Podborski	CAN	110
10	Christian Orlainsky	AUT	105
11	Joel Gaspoz	SUI	102
12	Leonhard Stock	AUT	97
13	Jarle Halsnes	NOR	96
14	Hans Enn	AUT	93
15	Jacques Luethy	SUI	84
16	Bruno Noeckler	ITA	79
17	Paul Frommelt	LIE	77
18	Peter Wirnsberger	AUT	73
	Valeri Tsyganov	SOV	73
20	Vladimir Andreev	SOV	72
21	Jean-Luc Fournier	SUI	62
	Boris Strel	JUG	62
23	Uli Spiess	AUT	56
24	Toni Buergler	SUI	55
25	Franz Gruber	AUT	53
26	Marc Girardelli	LUX	51
27	Herbert Plank	ITA	49
28	Piero Gros	ITA	48
	Gerhard Pfaffenbichler	AUT	48
30	Helmut Hoeflehner	AUT	47
31	Pirmin Zurbriggen	SUI	46
	Stig Strand	SWE	46
33	Bengt Fjaellberg	SWE	45
	Hannes Spiss	AUT	45
35	Gerhard Jaeger	AUT	44
36	Paolo de Chiesa	ITA	43
	Franz Heinzer	SUI	43
38	Ken Read	CAN	42
39	Wolfram Ortner	AUT	41
40	Franz Klammer	AUT	37
41	Josef Walcher	AUT	33
42	Erwin Resch	AUT	32
	Joze Kuralt	JUG	32
44	Siegfried Kerschbaumer	ITA	31
45	Paul Arne Skajem	NOR	28
46	Odd Soerli	NOR	27
	Werner Grissmann	AUT	27
48	Vladimir Makeev	SOV	26
49	Michael Veith	BRD	25
50	Conradin Cathomen	SUI	24
	Peter Popangelov	BUL	24
52	Dave Irwin	CAN	23
53	Even Hole	NOR	20
	David Murray	CAN	20

	Peter Patterson	USA	20
	Walter Vesti	SUI	20
57	Henri Mollin	BEL	18
58	Peter Luescher	SUI	17
59	Peter Mally	ITA	16
60	Silvano Meli	ITA	15
	Urs Raeber	SUI	15
	Peter Renoth	BRD	15
	Roberto Grigis	ITA	15
64	Toshihiro Kaiwa	JPN	14
65	Chris Kent	CAN	12
	Andy Mill	USA	12
	Doug Powell	USA	12
	Bohumir Zeman	TCH	12
	Erwin Josi	SUI	12
	Giuliano Giardini	ITA	12
71	Mike Farny	USA	11
	Torsten Jakobsson	SWE	11
73	Riccardo Foppa	ITA	10
	John Buxman	USA	10
	K Gattermann	BRD	10
	Lars-Goeran Halvarsson	SWE	10
	Christian Neureuther	BRD	10
	Hiroaki Ohtaka	JPN	10
79	Hubert Strolz	AUT	9
	Shinya Chiba	JPN	9
	Alex Giorgi	ITA	9
	Peter Roth	BRD	9
83	Frank Woerndl	BRD	8
	Kurt Gubser	SUI	8
85	Robert McKee	IRE	7
	Ernst Riedelsberger	AUT	7
87	Hubert Nachbauer	AUT	6
	Sepp Wildgruber	BRD	6
	Didier Bouvet	FRA	6
	Grega Benedik	JUG	6
91	Albert Burger	BRD	4
	Patrick Lamotte	FRA	4
	Alain Navillod	FRA	4
	Ivan Pacak	TCH	4
	Philippe Pugnat	FRA	4
	Marco Tonazzi	ITA	4
97	Miro Oberstar	JUG	3
98	Michel Canac	FRA	2
	Klaus Heidegger	BRD	2
	Gerard Rambaud	FRA	2
	Rune Saefvenberg	SWE	2
	Janez Zibler	JUG	2
103	Karl Anderson	USA	1
	Florian Beck	BRD	1
	Tomaz Cerkovnik	JUG	1
	Helmut Gstrein	AUT	1

1967

1	N Greene	CAN	176
2	M Goitschel	FRA	172
3	A Famose	FRA	158
4	I Mir	FRA	115
5	F Steurer	FRA	114
6	E Schinegger	AUT	110

1968

1	N Greene	CAN	191
2	I Mir	FRA	159
3	F Steurer	FRA	153
4	M Goitschel	FRA	128
5	F Bochatay	SUI	126
6	A Famose	FRA	123

1969

1	G Gabl	AUT	131
2	F Steurer	FRA	112
3	W Drexel	AUT	111
4	C Cutter	USA	107
5	I Lafforgue	FRA	103
6	A Famose	FRA	101

1970

1	M Jacot	FRA	180
2	F Macchi	FRA	145
3	F Steurer	FRA	133
4	I Lafforgue	FRA	132
5	B Cochran	USA	120
6	J Nagel	USA	118

1971

1	A-M Proell	AUT	210
2	M Jacot	FRA	177
3	I Mir	FRA	133
4	W Drexel	AUT	124
5	M Macchi	FRA	122
6	B Lafforgue	FRA	112

1972

1	A-M Proell	AUT	269
2	F Macchi	FRA	187
3	B Lafforgue	FRA	128
4	M Kaserer	AUT	120
5	M-T Nadig	SUI	111
6	R Mittermaier	BRD	110

1973

1	A-M Proell	AUT	297
2	M Kaserer	AUT	223
3	P Emonet	FRA	163

4	R Mittermaier	BRD	131
5	H Wenzel	LIE	112
6	W Drexel	AUT	106

1974

1	A-M Moser-Proell	AUT	268
2	M Kaserer	AUT	153
3	H Wenzel	LIE	144
4	C Zechmeister	BRD	129
5	F Serrat	FRA	127
6	M-T Nadig	SUI	123

1975

1	A-M Moser-Proell	AUT	305
2	H Wenzel	LIE	199
3	R Mittermaier	BRD	166
4	M-T Nadig	SUI	154
5	F Serrat	FRA	153
	B Zurbriggen	SUI	153

1976

1	R Mittermaier	BRD	281
2	L-M Morerod	SUI	214
3	M Kaserer	AUT	171
4	B Zurbriggen	SUI	170
5	D Debernard	FRA	164
6	B Totschnig	AUT	155

1977

1	L-M Morerod	SUI	319
2	A-M Moser-Proell	AUT	246
3	M Kaserer	AUT	196
4	B Habersatter	AUT	186
5	H Wenzel	LIE	150
6	M-T Nadig	SUI	133

1978

1	H Wenzel	LIE	154
2	A-M Moser-Proell	AUT	147
3	L-M Morerod	SUI	135
4	F Serrat	FRA	105
5	C Nelson	USA	97
6	P Pelen	FRA	96

1979

1	A-M Moser-Proell	AUT	243
2	H Wenzel	LIE	240
3	I Epple	BRD	189
4	C Nelson	USA	168
5	M-T Nadig	SUI	156
6	F Serrat	FRA	151

1980

1	H Wenzel	LIE	311
2	A-M Moser-Proell	AUT	259
3	M-T Nadig	SUI	221
4	P Pelen	FRA	192
5	I Epple	BRD	141
6	F Serrat	FRA	124
7	E Hess	SUI	109
8	C Giordani	ITA	107
9	D Zini	ITA	99
10	C Nelson	USA	98

1981

1	Marie-Therese Nadig	SUI	289
2	Erika Hess	SUI	251
3	Hanni Wenzel	LIE	241
4	Christine Cooper	USA	198
5	Irene Epple	BRD	181
6	Tamara McKinney	USA	176
	Perrine Pelen	FRA	176
8	Cindy Nelson	USA	168
9	Christa Kinshofer	BRD	165
10	Fabienne Serrat	FRA	149
11	Daniela Zini	ITA	137
12	Maria Walliser	SUI	112
13	Doris de Agostini	SUI	110
14	Maria Epple	BRD	102
15	Olga Charvatova	TCH	84
16	Cornelia Proell	AUT	78
17	Wanda Bieler	ITA	75
18	Maria Rosa Quario	ITA	64
19	Holly Beth Flanders	USA	63
20	Torill Fjelstad	NOR	62
21	Regine Moesenlechner	BRD	61
	Claudia Giordani	ITA	61
	Jana Soltysova	TCH	61
24	Zoe Haas	SUI	58
25	Traudl Haecher	BRD	55
26	Piera Macchi	ITA	52
27	Kathy Kreiner	CAN	49
	Nadezhda Patrakeeva	SOV	49
29	Abigail Fisher	USA	47
30	Heidi Preuss	USA	46
31	Gerry Sorensen	CAN	45
	Lea Soelkner	AUT	45
33	Elizabeth Kirchler	AUT	42
34	Brigitte Glur	SUI	37
35	Edith Peter	AUT	35
36	Marie-Luce Waldmeier	FRA	33
37	Marie-Cecile Gros-Gaudenier	FRA	32
38	Ursula Konsett	LIE	30
39	Cindy Oak	USA	25
40	Heidi Wiesler	BRD	22
41	Ingrid Eberle	AUT	21
	Bojana Dornig	JUG	21

	Elisabeth Chaud	FRA 21	57	Christine Klossner	SUI 6	Karen Lancaster	USA 3
44	Caroline Attia	FRA 20		Lorene Frigo	ITA 6	Corinne Eugster	SUI 3
45	Anne-Flore Rey	FRA 18		Sylviana Fabre	FRA 6	Brigitte Gadient	SUI 3
46	Petra Wenzel	LIE 17	60	Regina Sackl	AUT 5	Ariane Ehrat	SUI 3
	Michaela Gerg	BRD 17		Paoletta Magoni	ITA 5	Silvia Bonfini	ITA 3
48	Annemarie Bischofsberger	SUI 14		Andrea Haaser	AUT 5	76 Dorota Tlalka	POL 2
49	Anja Zavadlav	JUG 13		Rosi Aschenwald	AUT 5	Matka Jerman	JUG 2
	Roswitha Steiner	AUT 13	64	Annemarie Steiner	AUT 4	Diana Haight	CAN 2
51	Sylvia Eder	AUT 12		Andreja Leskovsek	JUG 4	Karin Unterseer	BRD 2
52	Brigitte Nansoz	SUI 11	66	Marianne Zechmeister	BRD 3	Inge Krenn	AUT 2
	Elisabeth Kraml	AUT 11		Catherine Quittet	FRA 3	81 Rita Naepflin	SUI 1
	Laurie Graham	CAN 11		Paola Marciandi	ITA 3	Maria Marichich	USA 1
	Erika Gfrerer	AUT 11		Ann Kronbichler	AUT 3	Monika Henkel	BRD 1
56	Natasa Blazic	JUG 8		Edith Lindner	AUT 3	Blanca Fernandez	SPA 1

NATIONS' CUP 1981

1	Switzerland	1584	8	USSR	421	15	Japan	33
2	Austria	1284	9	Sweden	399	16	Bulgaria	24
3	USA	1276	10	Canada	315	17	Belgium	18
4	Italy	738	11	Yugoslavia	302	18	Ireland	7
5	West Germany	723	12	Norway	253	19	Poland	2
6	Liechtenstein	519	13	Czechoslovakia	173	20	Spain	1
7	France	498	14	Luxemburg	57			

MEN

1	Austria	982	7	Yugoslavia	254	13	Japan	33
2	Switzerland	662	8	Liechtenstein	216	14	France	25
3	USA	517	9	Canada	208	15	Bulgaria	24
4	Sweden	399	10	Norway	191	16	Belgium	18
5	USSR	372	11	West Germany	88	17	Czechoslovakia	16
6	Italy	318	12	Luxemburg	57	18	Ireland	7

WOMEN

1	Switzerland	922	6	Liechtenstein	303	11	USSR	49
2	USA	759	7	Austria	302	12	Yugoslavia	48
3	West Germany	635	8	Czechoslovakia	157	13	Poland	2
4	France	473	9	Canada	208	14	Spain	1
5	Italy	420	10	Norway	62			

WORLD CUP RESULTS 1980-81

MEN/DOWNHILL

1980

1	P Mueller	SUI 96	W Grissmann	AUT 60	3 P Mueller	SUI	95
2	K Read	CAN 87	9 S Podborski	CAN 35	4 P Wirnsberger	AUT	73
3	H Plank	ITA 81	10 M Veith	BRD 28	5 U Spiess	AUT	56
4	H Weirather	AUT 75			6 V Tsyganov	SOV	55
5	E Haker	NOR 64	**1981**	**Pts**	T Buergler	SUI	55
6	P Wirnsberger	AUT 63			8 G Pfaffenbichler	AUT	48
7	J Walcher	AUT 60	1 H Weirather	AUT 115	9 H Hoeflehner	AUT	47
			2 S Podborski	CAN 110	10 F Heinzer	SUI	43

	L Stock	AUT	43
12	K Read	CAN	42
13	F Klammer	AUT	37
14	J Walcher	AUT	33
15	E Resch	AUT	32
16	H Plank	ITA	29
17	W Grissmann	AUT	27
18	V Makeev	SOV	26
19	C Cathomen	SUI	24
20	D Irwin	CAN	23
21	M Veith	BRD	21
22	P Patterson	USA	20
	D Murray	CAN	20
	W Vesti	SUI	20
25	U Raeber	SUI	15
	S Meli	SUI	15
27	D Powell	USA	12
	G Giardini	ITA	12
	A Mill	USA	12
	C Kent	CAN	12
	E Josi	SUI	12
32	P Mahre	USA	10
33	A Wenzel	LIE	9
34	P Luescher	SUI	7
35	H Nachbauer	AUT	6
36	P Pugnat	FRA	4
37	S Kerschbaumer	ITA	3
38	H Enn	AUT	2
	G Rambaud	FRA	2
40	K Anderson	USA	1

Val d'Isère France
7.12.80

1	Spiess	AUT	2:00.15
2	Read	CAN	2:00.52
3	Podborski	CAN	2:00.71
4	Kent	CAN	2:01.24
5	Irwin	CAN	2:01.33
6	Patterson	USA	2:01.36
7	Murray	CAN	2:01.48
8	Pfaffenbichler	AUT	2:01.51
9	Makeev	SOV	2:01.66
10	Vesti	SUI	2:01.92
11	Powell	USA	2:01.95
12	Pugnat	FRA	2:01.96
13	Tsyganov	SOV	2:02.06
14	Kerschbaumer	ITA	2:02.12
	Raeber	SUI	2:02.12

Val Gardena Italy
14.12.80

1	Mueller	SUI	2:01.24
2	Weirather	AUT	2:01.59
3	Podborski	CAN	2:02.00
4	Resch	AUT	2:02.07
5	Spiess	AUT	2:02.13
6	Stock	AUT	2:02.39
7	Josi	SUI	2:02.55
8	Hoeflehner	AUT	2:02.74
9	Luescher	SUI	2:02.81

10	Klammer	AUT	2:02.98
11	Read	CAN	2:03.13
	Veith	BRD	2:03.13
13	Vesti	SUI	2:03.23
14	Murray	CAN	2:03.33
15	Wenzel	LIE	2:03.35

Cortina d'Ampezzo Italy
15.12.80

1	Weirather	AUT	1:52.96
2	Spiess	AUT	1:53.09
3	Mueller	SUI	1:53.36
4	Mill	USA	1:53.80
5	Stock	AUT	1:53.88
6	Klammer	AUT	1:53.90
	Read	CAN	1:53.90
8	Veith	BRD	1:54.10
9	Buergler	SUI	1:54.25
10	Podborski	CAN	1:54.26
11	Murray	CAN	1:54.30
12	Resch	AUT	1:54.36
13	Plank	ITA	1:54.59
14	Vesti	SUI	1:54.68
15	Cathomen	SUI	1:54.74

St Moritz Switzerland
21.12.80

1	Podborski	CAN	1:54.31
2	Wirnsberger	AUT	1:54.41
3	Mueller	SUI	1:54.88
4	Tsyganov	SOV	1:54.92
5	Stock	AUT	1:54.99
6	Weirather	AUT	1:55.11
7	Walcher	AUT	1:55.23
8	Klammer	AUT	1:55.27
9	Read	CAN	1:55.36
10	Vesti	SUI	1:55.44
11	Irwin	CAN	1:55.56
12	Meli	SUI	1:55.66
13	Pfaffenbichler	AUT	1:55.71
14	Murray	CAN	1:55.82
15	Anderson	USA	1:55.86

Garmisch-Partenkirchen
West Germany
10.1.81

1	Podborski	CAN	1:55.48
2	Mueller	SUI	1:56.05
3	Weirather	AUT	1:56.31
4	Hoeflehner	AUT	1:56.71
5	Buergler	SUI	1:56.87
6	Plank	ITA	1:57.01
7	Wirnsberger	AUT	1:57.22
8	Veith	BRD	1:57.39
9	Resch	AUT	1:57.80
10	Raeber	SUI	1:57.98
11	Grissmann	AUT	1:58.09
12	Irwin	CAN	1:58.32
13	P Mahre	USA	1:58.34
14	Murray	CAN	1:58.35

| 15 | Klammer | AUT | 1:58.47 |

Kitzbuehel Austria
17.1.81

1	Podborski	CAN	2:03.76
2	Mueller	SUI	2:04.16
3	Wirnsberger	AUT	2:04.74
4	Plank	ITA	2:05.79
5	Weirather	AUT	2:05.83
6	Giardini	ITA	2:06.10
	Hoeflehner	AUT	2:06.10
8	Heinzer	SUI	2:06.13
9	P Mahre	USA	2:06.69
10	Grissmann	AUT	2:07.23
11	Walcher	AUT	2:07.29
12	Tsyganov	SOV	2:07.32
13	Raeber	SUI	2:07.43
14	Rambaud	FRA	2:07.83
15	Kerschbaumer	ITA	2:07.86

Wengen Switzerland
24.1.81

1	Buergler	SUI	2:27.91
2	Weirather	AUT	2:28.27
3	Podborski	CAN	2:28.46
4	Makeev	SOV	2:28.91
5	Tsyganov	SOV	2:28.92
6	Cathomen	SUI	2:29.17
7	Klammer	AUT	2:29.18
8	Walcher	AUT	2:29.21
9	Hoeflehner	AUT	2:29.22
10	Wirnsberger	AUT	2:29.25
11	Patterson	USA	2:29.39
12	Heinzer	SUI	2:29.40
13	Vesti	SUI	2:29.60
14	Josi	SUI	2:29.66
15	Raeber	SUI	2:29.82

St Anton Austria
31.1.81

1	Weirather	AUT	1:59.67
2	Wirnsberger	AUT	1:59.73
3	Podborski	CAN	2:00.15
4	Pfaffenbichler	AUT	2:00.18
5	Walcher	AUT	2:00.30
6	Cathomen	SUI	2:00.80
7	Heinzer	SUI	2:00.86
8	Wenzel	LIE	2:01.03
9	Makeev	SOV	2:01.05
10	Nachbauer	AUT	2:01.06
11	Hoeflehner	AUT	2:01.10
12	Plank	ITA	2:01.15
13	Raeber	SUI	2:01.21
14	Enn	AUT	2:01.42
15	Klammer	AUT	2:01.43

Aspen USA
5.3.81

| 1 | Tsyganov | SOV | 1:52.95 |

2	Weirather	AUT	1:53.11	13	Irwin	CAN	1:54.57	5	Mueller	SUI	1:53.05
3	Pfaffenbichler	AUT	1:53.18	14	Cathomen	SUI	1:54.68	6	Pfaffenbichler	AUT	1:53.20
4	Mueller	SUI	1:53.75	15	Klammer	AUT	1:54.85	7	Resch	AUT	1:53.50
5	Meli	SUI	1:53.78					8	Grissmann	AUT	1:53.62
6	Hoeflehner	AUT	1:53.82					9	Powell	USA	1:53.82
7	Wirnsberger	AUT	1:53.97					10	Stock	AUT	1:53.85
8	Grissmann	AUT	1:54.12					11	Hoeflehner	AUT	1:53.93
9	Heinzer	SUI	1:54.26					12	Klammer	AUT	1:54.05
10	Podborski	CAN	1:54.35					13	Wirnsberger	AUT	1:54.23
11	Patterson	USA	1:54.51					14	Giardini	ITA	1:54.45
	Stock	AUT	1:54.51					15	Cathomen	SUI	1:54.48

Aspen USA
6.3.81

1	Weirather	AUT	1:52.21
2	Podborski	CAN	1:52.49
3	Heinzer	SUI	1:52.59
4	Buergler	SUI	1:52.84

MEN/SLALOM

1980

1	I Stenmark	SWE	125
2	B Krizaj	JUG	88
3	C Neureuther	BRD	69
4	P Popangelov	BUL	64
5	A Zhirov	SOV	57
6	C Orlainsky	AUT	55
7	J Luethy	SUI	53
8	A Wenzel	LIE	51
9	A Steiner	AUT	49
10	P Frommelt	LIE	45

1981

			Pts
1	I Stenmark	SWE	120
2	P Mahre	USA	97
3	B Krizaj	JUG	80
	S Mahre	USA	80
5	P Frommelt	LIE	77
6	A Zhirov	SOV	70
7	W Andreev	SOV	62
8	P Gros	ITA	48
9	S Strand	SWE	46
	J Halsnes	NOR	46
11	B Fjaellberg	SWE	45
	F Gruber	AUT	45
13	C Orlainski	AUT	44
14	P de Chiesa	ITA	43
15	M Girardelli	LUX	40
16	J Gaspoz	SUI	31
17	A Wenzel	LIE	28
18	P Popangelov	BUL	24
19	B Noeckler	ITA	23
20	P Mally	ITA	16
21	R Grigis	ITA	15
22	T Kaiwa	JPN	14
23	O Soerli	NOR	11
	W Ortner	AUT	11
	J Luethy	SUI	11
26	L Halvarsson	SWE	10
	C Neureuther	BRD	10
	J Kuralt	JUG	10
	J Buxman	USA	10
30	H Enn	AUT	8
31	F Woerndl	BRD	7
32	K Gubser	SUI	6
	D Bouvet	FRA	6
34	M Tonazzi	ITA	4
	P Lamotte	FRA	4
36	K Heidegger	AUT	2
	M Canac	FRA	2
38	F Beck	BRD	1
	H Gstrein	AUT	1
	P A Skajem	NOR	1

Madonna di Campiglio Italy
9.12.80

1	Stenmark	SWE	1:41.05
2	Frommelt	LIE	1:41.62
3	Krizaj	JUG	1:41.76
4	Mally	ITA	1:42.06
5	Strand	SWE	1:43.18
6	de Chiesa	ITA	1:43.22
7	Gros	ITA	1:43.59
8	Gaspoz	SUI	1:44.13
9	Gruber	AUT	1:44.23
10	Bouvet	FRA	1:44.25
11	Orlainsky	AUT	1:44.48
12	Tonazzi	ITA	1:44.56
13	Grigis	ITA	1:44.45
14	Girardelli	LUX	1:44.60
15	Kaiwa	JPN	1:44.66

Garmisch-Partenkirchen
West Germany
11.1.81

1	S Mahre	USA	1:20.07
2	Popangelov	BUL	1:20.57
3	Frommelt	LIE	1:20.63
4	Krizaj	JUG	1:20.90
5	Gros	ITA	1:21.41
6	Neureuther	BRD	1:21.52
7	Strand	SWE	1:21.66
8	Noeckler	ITA	1:21.82
9	Woerndl	BRD	1:22.38
10	P Mahre	USA	1:22.40
11	Girardelli	LUX	1:22.82
12	Andreev	SOV	1:22.88
13	Kuralt	JUG	1:23.00
14	Canac	FRA	1:23.07
15	Beck	BRD	1:23.12

Oberstaufen West Germany
13.1.81

1	Frommelt	LIE	1:44.41
2	Stenmark	SWE	1:44.43
3	S Mahre	USA	1:44.78
4	P Mahre	USA	1:45.66
5	Orlainsky	AUT	1:45.71
6	Zhirov	SOV	1:46.45
7	Gros	ITA	1:46.48
8	Enn	AUT	1:46.87
9	Gruber	AUT	1:46.97
10	de Chiesa	ITA	1:46.99
11	Andreev	SOV	1:47.36
12	Krizaj	JUG	1:47.42
13	Kuralt	JUG	1:47.64
14	Heidegger	AUT	1:48.24
15	Strand	SWE	1:48.60

Kitzbuehel Austria
18.1.81

1	Stenmark	SWE	1:40.47
2	Andreev	SOV	1:41.41
3	Orlainsky	AUT	1:41.34
4	Grigis	ITA	1:41.46
5	Gaspoz	SUI	1:41.74
6	Strand	SWE	1:41.83
7	Halvarsson	SWE	1:41.87
8	Buxman	USA	1:42.31
9	Zhirov	SOV	1:42.37
10	Gubser	SUI	1:42.54
11	Girardelli	LUX	1:42.55
12	Kuralt	JUG	1:42.64
13	Kaiwa	JPN	1:42.76
	Fjaellberg	SWE	1:42.76
15	Gstrein	AUT	1:42.80

Wengen Switzerland
25.1.81

1	Krizaj	JUG	1:34.27
2	Girardelli	LUX	1:34.69
3	Stenmark	SWE	1:34.84
4	Zhirov	SOV	1:35.23
5	de Chiesa	ITA	1:35.29
6	Orlainsky	AUT	1:35.31
7	Strand	SWE	1:35.41

S Mahre	USA	1:35.41
9 Frommelt	LIE	1:35.46
10 Halsnes	NOR	1:35.50
11 P Mahre	USA	1:35.76
12 Gaspoz	SUI	1:35.80
13 Gros	ITA	1:35.93
14 Kaiwa	JPN	1:36.04
15 Gruber	AUT	1:36.08

St Anton Austria
1.2.81

1 Stenmark	SWE	1:40.94
2 P Mahre	USA	1:41.06
3 Halsnes	NOR	1:41.62
4 Andreev	SOV	1:41.64
5 Ortner	AUT	1:41.95
6 Soerli	NOR	1:41.97
7 de Chiesa	ITA	1:41.98
8 Krizaj	JUG	1:42.03
9 Strand	SWE	1:42.05
10 Kaiwa	JPN	1:42.07
11 Noeckler	ITA	1:42.42
12 Gruber	AUT	1:42.67
13 Zhirov	SOV	1:42.72
14 Luethy	SUI	1:42.88
15 Skajem	NOR	1:42.90

Oslo Norway
8.2.81

1 Stenmark	SWE	1:32.51
2 Fjaellberg	SWE	1:33.09
3 Andreev	SOV	1:33.16
4 P Mahre	USA	1:33.27
5 Zhirov	SOV	1:33.51
6 S Mahre	USA	1:33.80
7 Frommelt	LIE	1:34.03
8 Gros	ITA	1:34.07
9 Halsnes	NOR	1:34.63
10 Strand	SWE	1:34.86
11 Noeckler	ITA	1:34.87
12 de Chiesa	ITA	1:34.97
13 Orlainsky	AUT	1:35.05
14 Buxman	USA	1:35.08
15 Wenzel	LIE	1:35.38

Are Sweden
15.2.81

1 P Mahre	USA	1:34.36
2 Stenmark	SWE	1:34.39
3 Gruber	AUT	1:34.51
4 Fjaellberg	SWE	1:34.77
5 Gros	ITA	1:34.88
6 Andreev	SOV	1:34.92
7 Luethy	SUI	1:35.26
8 Frommelt	LIE	1:35.49
9 Strand	SWE	1:35.57
10 Halsnes	NOR	1:35.69
11 Gaspoz	SUI	1:35.79
12 Popangelov	BUL	1:36.10
Wenzel	LIE	1:36.10
14 Kaiwa	JPN	1:36.35
15 Halvarsson	SWE	1:36.43

Furano Japan
15.3.81

1 P Mahre	USA	1:36.97
2 Krizaj	JUG	1:37.21
3 Stenmark	SWE	1:37.46
4 Zhirov	SOV	1:37.84
5 Wenzel	LIE	1:38.13
6 S Mahre	USA	1:38.29
7 Gruber	AUT	1:38.42
8 Halsnes	NOR	1:38.69
9 de Chiesa	ITA	1:39.05
10 Strand	SWE	1:39.09
11 Andreev	SOV	1:39.22
12 Mally	ITA	1:39.24
13 Gaspoz	SUI	1:39.38
14 Gros	ITA	1:39.42
15 Kaiwa	JPN	1:39.72

Borovetz Bulgaria
25.3.81

1 Zhirov	SOV	1:52.34
2 S Mahre	USA	1:52.75
3 P Mahre	USA	1:53.17
4 Wenzel	LIE	1:53.85
5 Stenmark	SWE	1:54.11
6 Fjaellberg	SWE	1:54.45
7 Halsnes	NOR	1:54.47
8 Girardelli	LUX	1:54.54
9 Gruber	AUT	1:54.73
10 Krizaj	JUG	1:54.85
11 Noeckler	ITA	1:55.01
12 Lamotte	FRA	1:55.27
13 Strand	SWE	1:55.63
14 Gros	ITA	1:55.70
15 Soerli	NOR	1:55.73

MEN/GIANT SLALOM

1980

1 I Stenmark	SWE	125
2 H Enn	AUT	87
3 J Luethy	SUI	82
4 A Wenzel	LIE	71
5 J Gaspoz	SUI	68
6 B Krizaj	YUG	56
7 J Halsnes	NOR	51
8 B Strel	YUG	50
9 P Mahre	USA	43
10 B Zeman	TCH	42

1981

		Pts
1 I Stenmark	SWE	125
2 A Zhirov	SOV	115
3 P Mahre	USA	84
4 J Gaspoz	SUI	71
5 J-L Fournier	SUI	62
6 C Orlainsky	AUT	61
7 B Noeckler	ITA	56
8 J Luethy	SUI	53
9 H Enn	AUT	52
10 J Halsnes	NOR	50
11 S Mahre	USA	46
12 B Strel	JUG	45
H Spiess	AUT	45
14 G Jaeger	AUT	44
15 B Krizaj	JUG	40
16 A Wenzel	LIE	38
17 P Zurbriggen	SUI	35
18 L Stock	AUT	34
19 W Ortner	AUT	30
20 P A Skajem	NOR	27
21 O Soerli	NOR	16
22 J Kuralt	JUG	15
23 T Jakobsson	SWE	11
M Girardelli	LUX	11
25 R Foppa	ITA	10
V Andreev	SOV	10
27 H Strolz	AUT	9
A Giorgi	ITA	9
29 F Gruber	AUT	8
30 E Riedelsberger	AUT	7
31 A Burger	BRD	4
A Navillod	FRA	4
33 D Fontaine	FRA	3
34 K Gubser	SUI	2
35 V Tsyganov	SOV	1
F Woerndl	BRD	1

Madonna di Campiglio Italy
10.12.80

1 Stenmark	SWE	2:42.14
2 Zhirov	SOV	2:42.66
3 Jaeger	AUT	2:43.14
4 Enn	AUT	2:43.29
5 S Mahre	USA	2:43.48
6 Noeckler	ITA	2:43.54
7 Luethy	SUI	2:43.80
8 P Mahre	USA	2:43.84
9 Wenzel	LIE	2:43.93
10 Krizaj	JUG	2:44.13
11 Ortner	AUT	2:44.32
12 Navillod	FRA	2:44.50
13 Andreev	SOV	2:44.60

14	Orlainsky	AUT	2:44.61
15	Woerndl	BRD	2:44.63

Ebnat-Kappel Switzerland
4.1.81

1	Orlainsky	AUT	2:41.41
2	Enn	AUT	2:41.50
3	Fournier	SUI	2:41.58
4	P Mahre	USA	2:42.18
5	Spiss	AUT	2:42.32
6	Luethy	SUI	2:42.46
7	Wenzel	LIE	2:42.53
8	Noeckler	ITA	2:42.94
9	Gaspoz	SUI	2:42.95
10	Gruber	AUT	2:43.25
11	Jaeger	AUT	2:43.36
12	Halsnes	NOR	2:44.26
13	Ortner	AUT	2:44.75
	Riedelsberger	AUT	2:44.75
15	Kuralt	JUG	2:44.85

Morzine France
6.1.81

1	Stenmark	SWE	3:06.26
2	Gaspoz	SUI	3:06.77
3	Krizaj	JUG	3:06.83
4	P Mahre	USA	3:07.07
5	Noeckler	ITA	3:07.21
6	Wenzel	LIE	3:07.46
7	Zurbriggen	SUI	3:07.78
8	Stock	AUT	3:07.96
9	Luethy	SUI	3:08.03
10	Orlainsky	AUT	3:08.07
11	Zhirov	SOV	3:08.83
12	Skajem	NOR	3:09.33
13	Jaeger	AUT	3:09.54
14	Girardelli	LUX	3:09.97
15	Spiss	AUT	3:10.33

Adelboden Switzerland
26.1.81

1	Stenmark	SWE	2:45.00
2	Orlainsky	AUT	2:46.70
	Strel	JUG	2:46.70
4	Luethy	SUI	2:46.71
5	Halsnes	NOR	2:46.75
6	Zurbriggen	SUI	2:46.88
7	Fournier	SUI	2:46.93
8	P Mahre	USA	2:47.41
9	Wenzel	LIE	2:47.61
10	Noeckler	ITA	2:47.72
11	Kuralt	JUG	2:48.15
12	Skajem	NOR	2:48.39
13	Jakobsson	SWE	2:48.50
14	Gubser	SUI	2:49.00
15	Ortner	AUT	2:49.12

Schladming Austria
3.2.81

1	Stenmark	SWE	2:34.80
2	Enn	AUT	2:35.71
3	Fournier	SUI	2:35.82
4	Noeckler	ITA	2:35.86
5	Luethy	SUI	2:35.96
6	P Mahre	USA	2:36.02
7	Zhirov	SOV	2:36.72
8	Orlainsky	AUT	2:37.11
9	Halsnes	NOR	2:37.53
10	Strel	JUG	2:37.92
11	S Mahre	USA	2:38.15
12	Gaspoz	SUI	2:38.37
13	Krizaj	JUG	2:38.45
14	Gruber	AUT	2:39.08
15	Ortner	AUT	2:39.15

Voss Norway
11.2.81

1	Stenmark	SWE	3:08.60
2	Zhirov	SOV	3:10.09
3	Noeckler	ITA	3:11.42
4	Gaspoz	SUI	3:11.70
5	Halsnes	NOR	3:12.08
6	P Mahre	USA	3:12.21
7	Giorgi	ITA	3:12.63
8	Ortner	AUT	3:12.82
9	Spiss	AUT	3:12.84
10	Luethy	SUI	3:13.13
11	Kuralt	JUG	3:13.30
12	Zurbriggen	SUI	3:13.37
13	S Mahre	USA	3:13.48
14	Jakobsson	SWE	3:14.09
15	Strel	JUG	3:14.16

Are Sweden
14.2.81

1	Stenmark	SWE	2:40.96
2	Zhirov	SOV	2:42.43
3	P Mahre	USA	2:42.84
4	Fournier	SUI	2:43.80
5	Luethy	SUI	2:44.31
6	Soerli	NOR	2:44.80
7	Ortner	AUT	2:44.95
8	Halsnes	NOR	2:45.24
9	Skajem	NOR	2:45.47
10	Krizaj	JUG	2:45.57
11	S Mahre	USA	2:45.59
12	Riedelsberger	AUT	2:45.81
13	Wenzel	LIE	2:45.87
14	Strel	JUG	2:46.02
15	Foppa	ITA	2:46.03

Aspen USA
7.3.81

1	P Mahre	USA	3:12.76
2	Stenmark	SWE	3:12.90
3	S Mahre	USA	3:15.22

4	Gaspoz	SUI	3:15.30
5	Fournier	SUI	3:15.54
6	Zhirov	SOV	3:15.76
7	Girardelli	LUX	3:15.99
8	Noeckler	ITA	3:16.69
9	Spiss	AUT	3:16.86
10	Jakobsson	SWE	3:16.98
11	Wenzel	LIE	3:17.34
12	Krizaj	JUG	3:17.50
13	Strel	JUG	3:18.10
14	Soerli	NOR	3:18.27
15	Jaeger	AUT	3:18.38

Furano Japan
14.3.81

1	Zhirov	SOV	3:00.41
2	Jaeger	AUT	3:01.54
3	Stenmark	SWE	3:01.63
4	Gaspoz	SUI	3:01.94
5	Stock	AUT	3:02.04
6	Zurbriggen	SUI	3:02.12
7	Spiss	AUT	3:03.99
8	Luethy	SUI	3:04.14
9	Strel	JUG	3:04.45
10	Noeckler	ITA	3:04.47
11	Ortner	AUT	3:04.61
12	Kuralt	JUG	3:04.68
13	Fournier	SUI	3:04.81
14	Krizaj	JUG	3:04.96
15	Tsyganov	SOV	3:05.02

Borovetz Bulgaria
24.3.81

1	Zhirov	SOV	2:29.39
2	Stenmark	SWE	2:30.55
3	Gaspoz	SUI	2:30.67
4	Halsnes	NOR	2:31.05
5	P Mahre	USA	2:31.79
6	S Mahre	USA	2:32.68
7	Krizaj	JUG	2:32.77
8	Foppa	ITA	2:32.78
9	Strel	JUG	2:32.83
10	Spiss	AUT	2:32.91
11	Stock	AUT	2:33.12
12	Soerli	NOR	2:33.41
13	Noeckler	ITA	2:33.53
14	Zurbriggen	SUI	2:33.70
15	Strolz	AUT	2:33.73

Laax Switzerland
29.3.81

1	Zhirov	SOV	2:39.80
2	P Mahre	USA	2:40.05
3	Stenmark	SWE	2:40.24
4	Skajem	NOR	2:40.33
5	Spiss	AUT	2:41.13
6	Stock	AUT	2:41.23
7	Strolz	AUT	2:41.54
8	Halsnes	NOR	2:41.58
9	Andreev	SOV	2:42.01

10 Fournier	SUI	2:42.06	12 Burger	BRD	2:42.25	14 Zurbriggen	SUI	2:42.32
11 Strel	JUG	2:42.19	13 Gaspoz	SUI	2:42.27	15 Foppa	ITA	2:42.34

MEN/COMBINED

Val d'Isère/Ebnat-Kappel

1 Wenzel	LIE
2 Enn	AUT
3 P Mahre	USA
4 Luethy	SUI
5 Zurbriggen	SUI
6 Kerschbaumer	ITA
7 Strel	JUG
8 Farny	USA
9 Kuralt	JUG
10 Benedik	JUG
11 Wildgruber	BRD
12 Pacak	TCH
13 Oberstar	JUG
14 Zibler	JUG
15 Cerkovnik	JUG

Val Gardena

1 Mueller	SUI
2 Stock	AUT
3 Wenzel	LIE

4 P Mahre	USA
5 Enn	AUT
6 Luescher	SUI
7 S Mahre	USA
8 Luethy	SUI
9 Kerschbaumer	ITA
10 Tsyganov	SOV
11 Krizaj	JUG
12 Veith	BRD
13 Farny	USA
14 Saefvenberg	SWE
15 Wildgruber	BRD

Morzine/Garmisch-Partenkirchen

1 P Mahre	USA
2 Mueller	SUI
3 Wenzel	LIE
4 Krizaj	JUG
5 Kerschbaumer	ITA
6 Gattermann	BRD
7 Roth	BRD

8 Strel	JUG
9 McKee	IRE

Oberstaufen/Kitzbuehel

1 P Mahre	USA
2 S Mahre	USA
3 Stenmark	SWE
4 Zeman	TCH
5 Tsyganov	SOV
6 Ohtaka	JPN
7 Chiba	JPN
8 Hole	NOR
9 Mollin	BEL

St Anton

1 P Mahre	USA
2 Plank	ITA
3 Renoth	BRD
4 Hole	NOR
5 Mollin	BEL

WOMEN/DOWNHILL

1980		Pts
1 M-T Nadig	SUI	125
2 A Moser-Proell	AUT	100
3 H Wenzel	LIE	66
4 C Nelson	USA	59
5 J Soltysova	TCH	58
6 I Epple	BRD	51
7 H Preuss	USA	48
8 D de Agostini	SUI	47
9 E Mittermaier	BRD	42
10 L Graham	CAN	38

1981		Pts
1 M-T Nadig	SUI	120
2 D de Agostini	SUI	110
3 C Proell	AUT	78
4 I Epple	BRD	71
5 T Fjeldstad	NOR	62
6 J Soltysova	TCH	61
7 C Nelson	USA	60
H Flanders	USA	60
9 H Wenzel	LIE	42
E Kirchler	AUT	42
11 M Walliser	SUI	41
12 G Sorensen	CAN	39
13 E Peter	AUT	35
14 M-T Waldmeier	FRA	33
15 C Kreiner	CAN	32

M-C Gros-Gaudenier	FRA	32
17 R Mosenlechner	BRD	29
18 L Soelkner	AUT	26
19 H Preuss	USA	25
C Oak	USA	25
21 C Kinshofer	BRD	21
22 Z Haas	SUI	20
C Attia	FRA	20
24 I Eberle	AUT	17
25 T Haecher	BRD	16
26 A Bischofsberger	SUI	14
27 E Chaud	FRA	13
28 E Kraml	AUT	11
L Graham	CAN	11
S Eder	AUT	11
31 E Gfrerer	AUT	6
K Klossner	SUI	6
33 E Hess	SUI	5
34 A-M Steiner	AUT	4
35 A Ehrat	SUI	3
A Haaser	AUT	3
C Quittet	FRA	3
H Wiesler	BRD	3
M Zechmeister	BRD	3
E Linder	AUT	3
41 C Cooper	USA	2
42 M Marichich	USA	1

Val d'Isère France
3.12.80

1 Nadig	SUI	1:33.10
2 Kreiner	CAN	1:34.07
3 I Epple	BRD	1:34.77
4 Soelkner	AUT	1:34.99
5 Haas	SUI	1:35.03
6 Waldmeier	FRA	1:35.33
7 Proell	AUT	1:35.53
8 Attia	FRA	1:35.56
9 Walliser	SUI	1:35.77
10 Kinshofer	BRD	1:35.79
11 Hess	SUI	1:35.98
12 Haecher	BRD	1:36.00
13 Zechmeister	BRD	1:36.07
14 Eberle	AUT	1:36.09
Soltysova	TCH	1:36.09

Piancavallo Italy
12.12.80

1 Nadig	SUI	1:41.38
2 Fjeldstad	NOR	1:41.64
3 de Agostini	SUI	1:41.93
4 Bischofberger	SUI	1:42.11
5 Graham	CAN	1:42.19
6 Proell	AUT	1:42.92
7 Flanders	USA	1:43.25
8 Waldmeier	FRA	1:43.30

9 Peter	AUT	1:43.48
10 Soltysova	TCH	1:43.72
11 Nelson	USA	1:43.85
12 Gros-Gaudenier	FRA	1:43.98
13 Ehrat	SUI	1:44.00
14 Eberle	AUT	1:44.01
15 Marichich	USA	1:44.07

Altenmarkt Austria
17.12.80

1 Soltysova	TCH	1:25.11
2 de Agostini	SUI	1:25.19
3 Fjeldstad	NOR	1:25.36
4 Proell	AUT	1:25.41
5 I Epple	BRD	1:25.83
6 Soelkner	AUT	1:25.92
7 Eberle	AUT	1:26.11
Preuss	USA	1:26.11
9 Charvatova	TCH	1:26.22
10 Oak	USA	1:26.34
11 Flanders	USA	1:26.43
12 Nelson	USA	1:26.61
13 Gros-Gaudenier	FRA	1:26.65
14 Bischofberger	SUI	1:26.69
15 Peter	AUT	1:26.79

Pfronten West Germany
8.1.81

1 Proell	AUT	1:19.36
2 de Agostini	SUI	1:19.54
3 Flanders	USA	1:19.75
4 Peter	AUT	1:20.03
5 Nelson	USA	1:20.34
6 Oak	USA	1:20.38
I Epple	BRD	1:20.38
8 H Wenzel	LIE	1:20.41
9 Soltysova	TCH	1:20.54
10 Klossner	SUI	1:20.61
11 Kirchler	AUT	1:20.63
12 A Steiner	AUT	1:20.70
13 Wiesler	BRD	1:20.86
14 Nadig	SUI	1:20.99
15 Haecher	BRD	1:21.08

Schruns Austria
12.1.81

1 de Agostini	SUI	1:17.92
2 Nelson	USA	1:18.46
3 I Epple	BRD	1:18.78
4 Attia	FRA	1:18.84
5 Preuss	USA	1:19.08

6 H Wenzel	LIE	1:19.26
7 Peter	AUT	1:19.42
8 Soltysova	TCH	1:19.46
9 Chaud	FRA	1:19.48
10 Gfrerer	AUT	1:19.59
11 Oak	USA	1:19.60
12 Waldemeier	FRA	1:19.64
13 Kreiner	CAN	1:19.66
14 Lindner	AUT	1:19.81
15 Kraml	AUT	1:20.13

Crans-Montana Switzerland
19.1.81

1 Nadig	SUI	1:44.50
2 de Agostini	SUI	1:44.60
3 Kinshofer	BRD	1:45.05
4 Soltysova	TCH	1:45.32
5 Gros-Gaudenier	FRA	1:45.37
6 Kraml	AUT	1:45.58
7 Walliser	SUI	1:45.68
8 Flanders	USA	1:45.70
9 Nelson	USA	1:45.73
10 Waldmeier	FRA	1:45.77
11 Kirchler	AUT	1:45.85
12 Oak	USA	1:46.15
13 Proell	AUT	1:46.18
14 Quittet	FRA	1:46.20
15 Haecher	BRD	1:46.27

Megève France
28.1.81

1 de Agostini	SUI	1:21.20
2 Nadig	SUI	1:21.70
3 Fjeldstad	NOR	1:21.86
4 Flanders	USA	1:21.90
5 Proell	AUT	1:21.99
6 I Epple	BRD	1:22.01
7 Kreiner	CAN	1:22.11
8 Walliser	SUI	1:22.34
Haecher	BRD	1:22.34
10 Gros-Gaudenier	FRA	1:22.36
11 H Wenzel	LIE	1:22.42
12 Soltysova	TCH	1:22.46
13 Sorensen	CAN	1:22.57
14 Haas	SUI	1:22.87
15 Nelson	USA	1:23.02

Megève France
29.1.81

1 Nadig	SUI	1:21.05
2 de Agostini	SUI	1:21.13

3 Proell	AUT	1:21.69
4 Flanders	USA	1:22.06
5 Walliser	SUI	1:22.07
Sorensen	CAN	1:22.07
7 Soltysova	TCH	1:22.35
8 Gros-Gaudenier	FRA	1:22.49
9 Nelson	USA	1:22.68
10 Peter	AUT	1:22.75
11 Preuss	USA	1:22.80
12 H Wenzel	LIE	1:22.87
13 I Epple	BRD	1:22.89
14 Fjeldstad	NOR	1:22.97
15 Lindner	AUT	1:23.15

Haus Austria
8.2.81

1 Sorensen	CAN	1:39.27
2 I Epple	BRD	1:39.35
3 Proell	AUT	1:39.47
4 de Agostini	SUI	1:39.48
5 H Wenzel	LIE	1:39.60
6 Fjeldstad	NOR	1:39.65
7 Mosenlechner	BRD	1:39.70
8 Flanders	USA	1:39.75
9 Kirchler	AUT	1:39.78
10 Walliser	SUI	1:39.83
11 Nadig	SUI	1:39.90
12 Eberle	AUT	1:40.01
13 Haaser	AUT	1:40.26
14 Haecher	BRD	1:40.36
15 Waldmeier	FRA	1:40.44

Aspen USA
6.3.81

1 Kirchler	AUT	1:25.07
2 Moesenlechner	BRD	1:25.12
3 Nelson	USA	1:25.16
4 Flanders	USA	1:25.38
5 Eder	AUT	1:25.65
6 de Agostini	SUI	1:25.72
7 Nadig	SUI	1:25.77
8 H Wenzel	LIE	1:25.88
9 Haas	SUI	1:26.05
10 Chaud	FRA	1:26.16
11 Waldmeier	FRA	1:26.21
12 Soelkner	AUT	1:26.31
13 Gros-Gaudenier	FRA	1:26.58
14 Cooper	USA	1:26.75
15 Quittet	FRA	1:26.97

WOMEN/SLALOM

1980		Pts
1 P Pelen	FRA	120
2 H Wenzel	LIE	100
3 A Moser-Proell	AUT	88

4 D Zini	ITA	78
5 C Giordani	ITA	75
6 E Hess	SUI	62
7 F Serrat	FRA	56

8 R Moesenlechner	BRD	44
9 N Patrakeeva	SOV	43
10 T McKinney	USA	41
L Soelkner	AUT	41

1981

			Pts
1	E Hess	SUI	125
2	C Cooper	USA	86
3	D Zini	ITA	81
	P Pelen	FRA	81
5	F Serrat	FRA	63
6	H Wenzel	LIE	59
7	T McKinney	USA	52
8	P Macchi	ITA	51
9	N Patrakeeva	SOV	46
10	C Giordani	ITA	43
11	M R Quario	ITA	35
12	U Konzett	LIE	30
	B Glur	SUI	30
14	C Kinshofer	BRD	29
	A Fisher	USA	29
	C Nelson	USA	29
17	M Epple	BRD	28
18	O Charvatova	TCH	25
19	M Walliser	SUI	22
20	B Dornig	JUG	21
21	W Bieler	ITA	15
22	A F Rey	FRA	12
	A Zavadlav	JUG	12
24	B Nansoz	SUI	11
25	R Moesenlechner	BRD	10
26	N Blazic	JUG	8
	R Steiner	AUT	8
28	T Haecher	BRD	7
	M T Nadig	SUI	7
30	L Frigo	ITA	6
	S Fabre	FRA	6
32	R Sackl	AUT	5
	R Aschenwald	AUT	5
34	A Leskovsek	JUG	4
	I Eberle	AUT	4
36	L Soelkner	AUT	3
	P Magoni	ITA	3
	S Bonfini	ITA	3
39	K Unterseer	BRD	2
	D Tlalka	POL	2
41	R Naepflin	SUI	1
	I Epple	BRD	1
	P Marciandi	ITA	1

Piancavallo Italy
13.12.80

1	Serrat	FRA	1:51.85
2	Hess	SUI	1:52.98
3	Quario	ITA	1:53.26
4	Patrakeeva	SOV	1:53.50
5	Cooper	USA	1:53.77
6	Pelen	FRA	1:53.90
7	Dornig	JUG	1:54.77
8	Konzett	LIE	1:55.14
9	Fisher	USA	1:55.32
10	Fabre	FRA	1:55.36
11	McKinney	USA	1:55.46
12	Frigo	ITA	1:55.47

13	Haecher	BRD	1:55.66
14	Magoni	ITA	1:56.22
15	Marciandi	ITA	1:56.29

Altenmarkt Austria
18.12.80

1	Pelen	FRA	1:28.13
2	Kinshofer	BRD	1:28.35
3	Zini	ITA	1:28.43
4	Macchi	ITA	1:28.57
5	Serrat	FRA	1:28.58
6	Quario	ITA	1:28.99
7	Cooper	USA	1:29.11
8	Giordani	ITA	1:29.15
9	Patrakeeva	SOV	1:29.30
10	Nelson	USA	1:29.36
11	R Steiner	AUT	1:29.50
12	Eberle	AUT	1:30.08
13	Soelkner	AUT	1:30.13
14	Frigo	ITA	1:30.77
15	Magoni	ITA	1:31.04

Bormio Italy
20.12.80

1	Pelen	FRA	1:37.23
2	Patrakeeva	SOV	1:37.58
3	Hess	SUI	1:37.64
4	Konzett	LIE	1:37.65
5	Giordani	ITA	1:37.68
6	Cooper	USA	1:38.17
	Serrat	FRA	1:38.17
8	Nelson	USA	1:38.33
9	Dornig	JUG	1:38.49
10	Zavadlav	JUG	1:38.53
11	Fisher	USA	1:38.54
12	Glur	SUI	1:38.83
13	Bieler	ITA	1:38.84
14	M Epple	BRD	1:38.97
15	Naepflin	SUI	1:39.09

Schruns Austria
13.1.81

1	Hess	SUI	1:30.28
2	Giordani	ITA	1:32.01
3	McKinney	USA	1:32.04
4	H Wenzel	LIE	1:32.24
5	Zini	ITA	1:32.42
6	Cooper	USA	1:32.62
7	Moesenlechner	BRD	1:32.73
8	Macchi	ITA	1:32.83
9	Charvatova	TCH	1:33.32
10	Quario	ITA	1:33.51
11	Fisher	USA	1:33.81
12	Nelson	USA	1:35.30
13	Nansoz	SUI	1:36.01
14	Tlalka	POL	1:36.08

Crans-Montana Switzerland
21.1.81

1	Hess	SUI	1:33.46
2	Cooper	USA	1:33.90
3	H Wenzel	LIE	1:34.46
4	Fisher	USA	1:34.56
5	Zini	ITA	1:34.90
6	Konzett	LIE	1:35.19
7	Kinshofer	BRD	1:35.37
8	Macchi	ITA	1:36.37
9	Serrat	FRA	1:36.62
10	Charvatova	TCH	1:36.79
11	Glur	SUI	1:37.11
12	Nelson	USA	1:37.17
13	M Epple	BRD	1:37.83
14	Magoni	ITA	1:37.87
15	Marciandi	ITA	1:38.87

Les Diablerets Switzerland
21.1.81

1	Hess	SUI	1:17.98
2	Cooper	USA	1:18.84
3	Zini	ITA	1:18.87
4	Macchi	ITA	1:19.02
5	Pelen	FRA	1:19.41
6	Serrat	FRA	1:19.61
7	McKinney	USA	1:19.95
8	Nansoz	SUI	1:20.08
9	Glur	SUI	1:20.37
10	Zavadlav	JUG	1:20.45
11	Rey	FRA	1:20.77
12	Giordani	ITA	1:21.07
13	Bonfini	ITA	1:21.32
14	Sackl	AUT	1:21.35
15	Patrakeeva	SOV	1:21.42

Zwiesel West Germany
3.2.81

1	Hess	SUI	1:34.12
2	Zini	ITA	1:34.64
3	Cooper	USA	1:34.74
4	Charvatova	TCH	1:34.75
5	M Epple	BRD	1:34.92
6	H Wenzel	LIE	1:35.03
7	Bieler	ITA	1:35.12
8	Pelen	FRA	1:35.17
9	Walliser	SUI	1:35.35
10	Nadig	SUI	1:35.38
11	Aschenwald	AUT	1:35.57
12	Haecher	BRD	1:35.75
13	Sackl	AUT	1:35.91
14	Serrat	FRA	1:35.95
15	Moesenlechner	BRD	1:35.97

Furano Japan
15.3.81

1	Hess	SUI	1:19.18
2	Cooper	USA	1:19.36
3	M Epple	BRD	1:19.59

4	McKinney	USA	1:19.87
5	Macchi	ITA	1:20.43
6	H Wenzel	LIE	1:20.50
7	Pelen	FRA	1:21.06
8	Zini	ITA	1:21.12
9	Nelson	USA	1:21.21
10	Patrakeeva	SOV	1:21.28
11	Glur	SUI	1:21.90
12	Quario	ITA	1:22.02
13	Bieler	ITA	1:22.24
14	Serrat	FRA	1:22.52
15	Nadig	SUI	1:22.67

Wangs Switzerland
24.3.81

1	Hess	SUI	1:29.96
2	Zini	ITA	1:31.09
3	Walliser	SUI	1:31.44
4	H Wenzel	LIE	1:31.75
5	McKinney	USA	1:31.81
6	Pelen	FRA	1:32.04
7	Glur	SUI	1:32.28
8	Blazic	JUG	1:32.88
9	Serrat	FRA	1:33.32
10	Rey	FRA	1:33.80
11	Dornig	JUG	1:33.95
12	Leskovsek	JUG	1:33.96
13	R Steiner	AUT	1:34.29
14	Unterseer	BRD	1:34.56
15	I Epple	BRD	1:35.16

WOMEN/GIANT SLALOM

1980

			Pts
1	H Wenzel	LIE	125
2	P Pelen	FRA	95
	M-T Nadig	SUI	95
4	I Epple	BRD	83
5	E Hess	SUI	71
6	F Serrat	FRA	55
7	C Giordani	ITA	44
	A Moser-Proell	AUT	44
9	C Kinshofer	BRD	42
10	D Zini	ITA	37

1981

			Pts
1	T McKinney	USA	102
2	M-T Nadig	SUI	97
3	E Hess	SUI	78
	H Wenzel	LIE	78
	I Epple	BRD	78
6	M Epple	BRD	71
7	C Cooper	USA	69
8	C Kinshofer	BRD	63
9	P Pelen	FRA	60
	W Bieler	ITA	60
11	D Zini	ITA	56
12	C Nelson	USA	48
13	F Serrat	FRA	45
14	O Charvatova	TCH	31
15	M R Quario	ITA	29
16	T Haecher	BRD	19
17	C Giordani	ITA	18
18	M Walliser	SUI	14
	Z Haas	SUI	14
20	M Gerg	BRD	13
21	A Kronbichler	AUT	10
22	P Wenzel	LIE	9
23	E Chaud	FRA	8
24	B Glur	SUI	7
25	A F Rey	FRA	6
	L Soelkner	AUT	6
	H Wiesler	BRD	6
28	R Moesenlechner	BRD	5
	R Steiner	AUT	5
30	K Lancaster	USA	3
	K Kreiner	CAN	3
	C Eugster	SUI	3
	N Patrakeeva	SOV	3
34	H Preuss	USA	2
	G Sorensen	CAN	2
36	P Marciandi	ITA	1
	P Macchi	ITA	1
	E Gfrerer	AUT	1
	B Fernandez	SPA	1
	I Krenn	AUT	1

Val d'Isère France
4.12.80

1	I Epple	BRD	2:16.92
2	Pelen	FRA	2:17.49
3	Kinshofer	BRD	2:17.72
4	Serrat	FRA	2:18.61
5	Nadig	SUI	2:18.98
6	McKinney	USA	2:19.30
7	P Wenzel	LIE	2:19.50
8	Zini	ITA	2:19.83
9	Charvatova	TCH	2:19.97
10	Hess	SUI	2:20.10
11	Gerg	BRD	2:20.21
12	Nelson	USA	2:20.33
13	Quario	ITA	2:20.43
14	Soelkner	AUT	2:20.89
15	M Epple	BRD	2:20.97

Limone Piemonte Italy
7.12.80

1	Nadig	SUI	2:50.45
2	Zini	ITA	2:50.57
3	Serrat	FRA	2:50.76
4	Bieler	ITA	2:51.41
5	Hess	SUI	2:51.84
6	Pelen	FRA	2:51.98
7	Quario	ITA	2:52.10
8	Cooper	USA	2:52.69
9	Giordani	ITA	2:53.20
10	Haas	SUI	2:53.52
11	Walliser	SUI	2:53.67
12	Soelkner	AUT	2:54.79
13	Lancaster	USA	2:54.90
14	Kreiner	CAN	2:55.06
15	Marciandi	ITA	2:55.27

Haute-Nendaz Switzerland
22.1.81

1	McKinney	USA	2:35.09
2	H Wenzel	LIE	2:35.53
3	I Epple	BRD	2:35.60
4	Cooper	USA	2:35.87
5	Nadig	SUI	2:35.93
6	Bieler	ITA	2:37.05
7	Zini	ITA	2:37.36
8	Kinshofer	BRD	2:37.62
9	Kronbichler	AUT	2:38.29
10	Nelson	USA	2:38.31
11	Pelen	FRA	2:38.50
12	Giordani	ITA	2:38.96
13	Moesenlechner	BRD	2:39.07
14	Hess	SUI	2:39.08
15	Haas	SUI	2:39.24

Les Gets France
24.1.81

1	McKinney	USA	2:05.96
2	Kinshofer	BRD	2:07.65
3	H Wenzel	LIE	2:08.88
4	M Epple	BRD	2:08.76
5	Bieler	ITA	2:08.99
6	Zini	ITA	2:08.92
7	Pelen	FRA	2:09.12
8	Quario	ITA	2:09.53
9	Giordani	ITA	2:09.96
10	Nadig	SUI	2:10.36
11	Serrat	FRA	2:11.29
12	Nelson	USA	2:11.48
13	Charvatova	TCH	2:11.56
14	Preuss	USA	2:11.92
15	Macchi	ITA	2:12.11

Zwiesel West Germany
4.2.81

1	M Epple	BRD	2:18.69
2	Kinshofer	BRD	2:18.83
3	McKinney	USA	2:19.04
4	Bieler	ITA	2:19.53
5	Cooper	USA	2:19.66
6	Nadig	SUI	2:19.86
7	Pelen	FRA	2:19.91

8 H Wenzel	LIE	2:20.25	
9 Serrat	FRA	2:21.12	
10 Wiesler	BRD	2:21.26	
11 I Epple	BRD	2:21.27	
12 Gerg	BRD	2:21.42	
13 Kronbichler	AUT	2:21.95	
14 Hess	SUI	2:22.00	
15 Fernandez	SPA	2:22.21	

Maribor Yugoslavia
10.2.81

1 Nadig	SUI	2:31.40
2 M Epple	BRD	2:32.01
3 I Epple	BRD	2:32.16
4 Hess	SUI	2:32.23
5 Cooper	USA	2:32.45
6 Nelson	USA	2:33.11
7 McKinney	USA	2:33.36
8 H Wenzel	LIE	2:33.58
9 Haas	SUI	2:34.33
10 Rey	FRA	2:34.57
11 Pelen	FRA	2:34.66
12 Walliser	SUI	2:34.74
13 Charvatova	TCH	2:35.08
14 Moesenlechner	BRD	2:35.39
15 Gfrerer	AUT	2:35.63

Aspen USA
8.3.81.

1 McKinney	USA	2:23.59
2 Hess	SUI	2:24.09
3 Bieler	ITA	2:25.16
4 Pelen	FRA	2:25.86
5 Nelson	USA	2:26.26
6 Haecher	BRD	2:26.40
7 Zini	ITA	2:26.48
8 I Epple	BRD	2:26.51
9 M Epple	BRD	2:26.66
10 Quario	ITA	2:26.77
11 Serrat	FRA	2:26.95
12 H Wenzel	LIE	2:26.98
13 Patrakeeva	SOV	2:27.23
14 Cooper	USA	2:27.32
15 Charvatova	TCH	2:27.56

Furano Japan
13.3.81

1 Nadig	SUI	2:34.05
2 H Wenzel	LIE	2:34.44
3 Cooper	USA	2:34.86
4 McKinney	USA	2:36.72
5 I Epple	BRD	2:37.16
6 Hess	SUI	2:37.22

Nelson	USA	2:37.22
8 Charvatova	TCH	2:37.69
9 Glur	SUI	2:38.12
10 M Epple	BRD	2:39.00
11 Walliser	SUI	2:39.39
12 Serrat	FRA	2:39.72
13 Quario	ITA	2:40.11
14 Sorensen	CAN	2:40.71
15 Kreiner	CAN	2:41.36

Wangs Switzerland
25.3.81

1 Hess	SUI	2:20.46
2 Cooper	USA	2:21.54
3 H Wenzel	LIE	2:21.79
4 I Epple	BRD	2:22.51
5 Nelson	USA	2:23.42
6 Charvatova	TCH	2:23.47
7 Haecher	BRD	2:24.72
8 Chaud	FRA	2:25.16
9 M Epple	BRD	2:25.59
10 Serrat	FRA	2:25.96
11 R Steiner	AUT	2:26.80
12 Gerg	BRD	2:27.00
13 Eugster	SUI	2:27.05
14 Bieler	ITA	2:27.31
15 Krenn	AUT	2:27.90

WOMEN/COMBINED

Val d'Isère

1 Nadig	SUI
2 I Epple	BRD
3 Kinshofer	BRD
4 Pelen	FRA
5 Serrat	FRA
6 Soelkner	AUT
7 Haas	SUI
8 Hess	SUI
9 Kreiner	CAN
10 P Wenzel	LIE
11 Nelson	USA
12 Gerg	BRD
13 Charvatova	TCH
14 McKinney	USA
15 Haecher	BRD

Limone Piemonte/Piancavallo

1 Nadig	SUI
2 Serrat	FRA
3 Hess	SUI
4 Pelen	FRA
5 Cooper	USA
6 Nelson	USA
7 Walliser	SUI
8 Haas	SUI
9 Kreiner	CAN
10 Preuss	USA

11 Wiesler	BRD
12 Sorensen	CAN
13 Haecher	BRD
14 Haight	CAN
15 Henkel	BRD

Crans-Montana

1 Kinshofer	BRD
2 Hess	SUI
3 Cooper	USA
4 H Wenzel	LIE
5 Nelson	USA
6 Serrat	FRA
7 Nadig	SUI
8 Charvatova	TCH
9 Fisher	USA
10 Walliser	SUI
11 Wiesler	BRD
12 I Epple	BRD
13 Gadient	SUI
14 Jerman	JUG
15 Zavadlav	JUG

Les Gets/Megève

1 H Wenzel	LIE
2 McKinney	USA
3 Nadig	SUI
4 Kinshofer	BRD

5 Pelen	FRA
6 Nelson	USA
7 Serrat	FRA
8 Preuss	USA
9 Haas	SUI
10 Moesenlechner	BRD
11 Fisher	USA
12 Gfrerer	AUT
13 Flanders	USA
14 Haaser	AUT
15 Krenn	AUT

Zwiesel/Haus

1 H Wenzel	LIE
2 Walliser	SUI
3 Cooper	USA
4 Nadig	SUI
5 Moesenlechner	BRD
6 Charvatova	TCH
7 Haecher	BRD
8 Hess	SUI
9 I Epple	BRD
10 Fisher	USA
11 Preuss	USA
12 Nelson	USA
13 Wiesler	BRD
14 P Wenzel	LIE
15 Eder	AUT

WORLD CUP CALENDAR 1981-1982

Oberstaufen

SWITZERLAND

Wengen **W**
Adelboden **M** **M** **•** Grindelwald
Morzine **•** **M**
Crans-Montana
M
Arosa
W

St Gervais **•** **•** Chamonix
W **W**

FRANCE
W **•** Pila
• Val d'Isère
W **M**

Aprica
M

Madonn
Campi

W **W**
M
• Sansicario
Montgenèvre

M Men's events
W Women's events

ITALY

WOMEN

Val d'Isère				Maribor				Oberstaufen	
1981 **2** DEC	1981 **3** DEC	🎿	🏁	1982 **3** JAN	1982 **4** JAN	🏁	🏁	1982 **9** FEB	🏁

Pila		Pfronten				Arosa			
1981 **6** DEC	🏁	1982 **8** JAN	1982 **9** JAN	🎿	🏁	1982 **13** FEB	1982 **14** FEB	🎿	🎿

Limone		Grindelwald				Winter Park			
1981 **7** DEC	🏁	1982 **13** JAN	1982 **14** JAN	🎿	🏁	1982 **25** FEB	1982 **26** FEB	🏁	🏁

Piancavallo				Bad Gastein				Aspen	
1981 **12** DEC	1981 **13** DEC	🎿	🏁	1982 **19** JAN	1982 **20** JAN	🎿	🏁	1982 **28** FEB	🏁

Bad Kleinkircheim				Lenggries		Waterville			
1981 **19** DEC	1981 **20** DEC	🎿	🎿	1982 **22** JAN	🏁	1982 **3** MAR	1982 **4** MAR	🏁	🏁

Chamonix/St Gervais				Berchtesgaden		Sansicario/Montgenèvre			
1981 **21** DEC	1981 **22** DEC	🏁	🏁	1982 **23** JAN	🏁	1982 **25** MAR	~ 1982 **28** MAR	🏁	🏁

World Cup Combined – Women
1. Val d'Isère — Downhill – Giant slalom
2. Limone/Piancavallo — Special slalom – Downhill
3. Pfronten/Grindelwald — Downhill – Giant slalom
4. Bad Gastein — Downhill – Special slalom

🏁 Special slalom   🎿 Downhill

🏁 Giant slalom

Bad Wiessee

Pfronten

GERMANY

Garmisch-
Partenkirchen • Lenggries

AUSTRIA

Berchtesgaden •

Kitzbuehel •

Schladming •

Bad Gastein •

Val Gardena

Cortina

Piancavallo

Bad Kleinkircheim

Kransjka Gora •

YUGOSLAVIA

Maribor •

Jasna
CZECHOSLOVAKIA

Main map

Limone
ITALY

CANADA
Mt Whistler   Waterville

USA

Aspen   Winter Park

MEN

Val d'Isère	Morzine	Mt Whistler
1981 4 DEC 1981 5 DEC	1982 9 JAN 1982 10 JAN	1982 27 FEB
Aprica	**Bad Wiessee**	**Aspen**
1981 8 DEC	1982 12 JAN	1982 5 MAR 1982 6 MAR
Madonna di Campiglio	**Kitzbuehel**	**Bad Kleinkircheim**
1981 9 DEC	1982 16 JAN 1982 17 JAN	1982 17 MAR
Val Gardena	**Adelboden**	**Kransjka Gora**
1981 13 DEC	1982 19 JAN	1982 19 MAR 1982 20 MAR
Cortina	**Wengen**	**Jasna**
1981 14 DEC 1981 15 DEC	1982 23 JAN 1982 24 JAN	1982 22 MAR 1982 23 MAR
Crans-Montana	**Garmisch-Partenkirchen**	**Sansicario/Montgenèvre**
1981 20 DEC	1982 13 FEB 1982 14 FEB	1982 25 MAR ~ 1982 28 MAR

World Cup Combined – Men

1. Val d'Isère   Downhill – Giant slalom
2. Madonna/Val Gardena   Special slalom – Downhill
3. Bad Wiessee/Kitzbuehel Special slalom – Downhill
4. Adelboden/Wengen   Giant slalom – Downhill
5. Garmisch-Partenkirchen Downhill – Special slalom

EUROPA CUP/MEN 1981-2

1981			Dh	Sl	GS	Comb.
19–20 December	Laax	SUI	XX			
1982						
9–10 January	Innsbruck	AUT	X	X		X
16–17 January	Sestrière	FRA	X		X	X
22–23 January	Méribel	FRA	XX			X
27–28 January	Valloire	FRA	XX			X
30–31 January	Tarvisio	ITA		X	X	X
3–4 February	Mehlmeisl	BRD		XX		X
24–25 February	Sarajevo	JUG		X	X	
28 February						
–1 March	Borovetz	BUL		X	X	
3–4 March		JUG		X	X	
6–7 March	Altenmarkt	AUT		X	X	
11–12 March	Diemtigen	SUI		X	X	
16–17 March	Valcarlina	ITA		X	X	
19–21 March	Villars de Lans	FRA		X	X	

EUROPA CUP/WOMEN 1981-2

1981			Dh	Sl	GS	Comb.
12–13 December	Zinal	SUI		X	X	X
18–19 December	Pra Loup	FRA	XX			X
1982						
9–10 January	Arnoldstein	AUT	XX			
16–17 January	Valzoldana	ITA	X	X		X
23 January	Megève	FRA	X			X
24–25 January	Les Gets	FRA		X	X	X
27–28 January	Meiringen	FRA		X	X	
2–3 February	Abetone	ITA		X	X	
5–6 February	Bled/Kranj	JUG		X	X	
8 February	Ljubljana	JUG		X		
27–28 February	Villach/Kleinkircheim	AUT		X	X	
6–7 March	Sarajevo	JUG	X		X	
10 March	Melette Gallio	ITA			X	
13–14 March	Valcarlina	ITA		X	X	
18–20 March	Villars de Lans	FRA		X	X	

SKI JUMPING WORLD CUP 1981-2

1981			70-metre	90-metre	120-metre	
20 December	Cortina	ITA	X			
30 December	Oberstdorf	BRD		X		
1982						4 Hills
1 January	Garmisch-Partenkirchen	BRD		X		Tournament
3 January	Innsbruck	AUT		X		
6 January	Bischofshofen	AUT		X		
9–10 January	St Nizier	FRA	XX			
15–17 January	Sapporo	JPN	X	X		
23–24 January	Thunder Bay	CAN	X	X		
27–31 January	St Moritz, Gstaad, Engelberg	SUI	X	X		
19–28 February	Oslo World Nordic Championships	NOR	X	X		
6–7 March	Lahti	FIN	X	X		
12–14 March	Kulm-Mitterndorf	AUT			X	
20–21 March	Strbske Pleso	TCH	X	X		
27–28 March	Planica	JUG	X	X		